W9-AZR-235

STEPS TO SUCCESS
FROM
TAKING CHARGE ON THE JOB

> "Most people are usually so wrapped up in worrying about being criticized that they miss the opportunity to find out what's going on. They apologize and hang their heads and walk away not really knowing what they did wrong, or how to correct it—or even how much or how little it means to the boss. Sometimes they end up with vague feelings of inadequacy; this only serves to make them more hesitant to show the boss their next project or idea."

> "Don't be unduly concerned over what's *fair*. It may not be *fair* that another manager is earning $5,000 more than you, but if that's what he was able to negotiate for—good for him. If you can negotiate for an equivalent increase—more power to you, too. If you don't get it, there's no point in pining over the 'unfairness' of it. Look around you; a lot of things in life are not meted out according to what's fair."

> "A rational approach to life is one that considers all variables. People who push logic or rationality often are simply pushing their own brand of reasoning. A true rationality considers the emotions and other 'illogical' input—even if irrational—because these factors matter. They are influential; they move people."

> "You want something. You ask for it. The other person says 'no.' You ask again. And again. And again. Eventually it will mean more to him to get rid of you than to keep you from getting what you want."

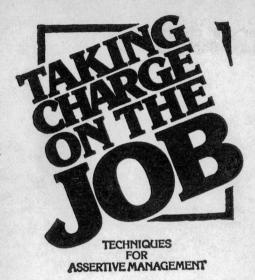

TAKING CHARGE ON THE JOB

TECHNIQUES FOR ASSERTIVE MANAGEMENT

LYN TAETZSCH & EILEEN BENSON

Edited by Robert Freiberg

BALLANTINE BOOKS • NEW YORK

For our children—
Blixy, Scott, and Kathy.

Library of Congress Catalog Card Number: 79-90560

ISBN 0-345-28720-7

This edition published by arrangement with
Executive Enterprises Publications Co., Inc.

Manufactured in the United States of America

First Ballantine Books Edition: April 1980

ACKNOWLEDGMENTS

George Kinney's encouragement helped Eileen Benson start a career that changed her life and ultimately led to the writing of this book.

Cassie Miller, Director of University College at Rutgers University, gave Eileen Benson her first job running assertiveness workshops.

Ellen Mittman, Public Relations Coordinator at Bamberger's Department Store in Paramus, New Jersey, and Myrna Masoff, Director of Future Events at A & S Department Store in Brooklyn, were also receptive to the idea of assertiveness training and helped make it possible for hundreds of women to attend Eileen Benson's workshops.

For help in the development of ideas and examples in this book we thank Debra Dewald, Adrian Epstein, Herb Genfan, Richard Samson, and Laura Taetzsch. They provided a sounding board for our ideas, shared their on-the-job experiences, and helped work out the kinks in our first drafts.

While there isn't room to name them, we sincerely thank all our students for the knowledge and experience they have shared with us.

Finally, we thank Bob Freiberg for his sensitive and thorough editing.

CONTENTS

INTRODUCTION

As a manager, most of your day is probably spent talking, listening, writing, or reading. You're either trying to understand someone else's message or to send one of your own. When you're on the sending end, you're often trying to get someone to do something. In a nutshell, this book is about how to do that successfully.

People find it difficult to express their needs and wants effectively. They don't want to aggressively step on other people's toes, yet they don't want to compliantly give in to everyone around them, either. That is why assertiveness training has become so popular.

Assertiveness is a two-way communication process for negotiating honestly with the people around you. It's a way to ask for what you want while still respecting the rights and needs of others. And it's an approach to life that says, "I am worthwhile and my needs are important."

Managers are continually put in positions where they have to negotiate—with subordinates, superiors, and peers. They must be able to get people to do things that need to be done.

On the next pages there is a short exercise that will show you how assertive a manager you are, where your strengths and weaknesses are. It will also give you an idea of some of the problems that this book covers—and will help you solve.

Assertiveness training is so effective because the verbal techniques can be learned quickly and used in everyday situations. The principles and practices in this book have helped many people to become better managers—of their work and of their lives. You may not need every chapter, but we promise that *some part* of this book will be of great value to you.

The Idea

HOW ASSERTIVE A MANAGER ARE YOU?

What is your most likely response to each of these situations?

1. When there's an unpleasant job that has to be done, I . . .
   - __ a. do it myself
   - __ b. give it as punishment to someone who's been goofing off
   - __ c. hesitate to ask a subordinate to do it
   - __ d. ask someone to do it just the same
2. When the boss criticizes me, I . . .
   - __ a. feel bad
   - __ b. show him where he's wrong
   - __ c. try to learn from it
   - __ d. apologize for being stupid
3. When an employee isn't working out, I . . .
   - __ a. give him room to hang himself
   - __ b. do everything I can to help him before firing him
   - __ c. put off firing him as long as possible
   - __ d. get rid of him as quickly as possible
4. When my raise isn't as large as I think it should be, I . . .
   - __ a. tell the boss in no uncertain terms what to do with it
   - __ b. keep quiet about it
   - __ c. say nothing, but take it out on the boss in other ways
   - __ d. tell the boss why I think I deserve a bigger raise

1

5. When a subordinate continues to ignore instructions after I've told him something for the third time, I . . .
___ a. try to give him something else to do
___ b. keep telling him until he does it
___ c. tell him if he doesn't do it right this time, he's out the door
___ d. try to explain it a different way

6. When the boss rejects a good idea of mine, I . . .
___ a. ask him why
___ b. walk away and feel bad
___ c. try it again later
___ d. think about joining the competition

7. When a co-worker criticizes me, I . . .
___ a. give him back twice what he gave me
___ b. avoid him in the future
___ c. don't care
___ d. worry that he doesn't like me

8. When someone tells a joke I don't get, I . . .
___ a. laugh with the rest of the group
___ b. tell him it was a lousy joke
___ c. tell him I didn't get it
___ d. feel stupid

9. When someone points out a mistake I've made, I . . .
___ a. sometimes deny it
___ b. feel guilty as hell
___ c. figure it's only human to make mistakes now and then
___ d. dislike the person for pointing it out

10. When a subordinate fouls up a job, I . . .
___ a. blow up
___ b. hate to tell him about it
___ c. try to figure out what went wrong
___ d. don't give him that job to do again

11. When I have to talk to a top executive, I . . .
___ a. can't look him in the eye
___ b. feel uncomfortable
___ c. get a little nervous
___ d. enjoy the interchange

12. When a subordinate asks me for a favor, I . . .
___ a. sometimes grant it, sometimes not
___ b. feel uncomfortable if I don't grant it

    __ c. usually refuse, otherwise it sets a bad prece-
         dent
    __ d. always give in

How Do You Rate Yourself?

1. The compliant or "nice-guy"* manager hates to ask people to do the unpleasant jobs and usually winds up doing them himself; the aggressive manager might assign such tasks as punishment; (d) is the assertive choice.

2. The aggressive manager argues with the boss when he's criticized. Feeling bad or guilty, while common, is a nonassertive feeling. Apologizing for "being stupid" is a self-degrading response. The assertive response is to try to learn from valid criticism.

3. The hard-nosed, authoritarian manager would get rid of a "bad" employee as quickly as possible. The nice guy would put it off as long as he could (possibly forever), or else give the employee room to hang himself in order to feel justified in firing him. The assertive manager does everything possible to help the employee, but fires him if that is finally necessary.

4. When people don't like a situation but say nothing about it, resentment builds up in them. It often leaks out into passive aggression—they "get back" in devious ways. Choice (a) is an aggressive reaction. Choice (d) is the assertive response.

5. Both (b) and (d) are assertive choices. Giving the employee something else to do is evading the responsibility. Threatening him is the hard-guy approach.

6. Planning to join the competition is passive aggression: "I'll get back at him—he'll be sorry!" Choices (a) and (c) are assertive ways to handle the situation; (b) is nonassertive, compliant behavior.

7. Giving better than you get (a) is aggressive behavior. By contrast, (b) and (d) are nonassertive

---

* There are nice-*guy* managers, and there are nice-*gal* managers. This book is about men and women, and it is addressed to both. And rather than have you read an awkward *he/she* or *his/her* throughout the pages that follow, we merely ask you to note that whenever we say *he* or *his,* we also mean *she* and *hers.*

3

choices. An assertive person wouldn't care about petty criticism from a co-worker. If the criticism is worthwhile, he'll take the advice. Effective ways of handling criticism are discussed in this book.

8. Both (a) and (d) are nonassertive responses. The assertive person is not afraid to say he didn't get the joke. The aggressive person blames the guy or gal for telling a lousy joke.

9. When someone points out a mistake we have made, common reactions are to feel guilty, to dislike the person for telling us about it, and perhaps even to deny we did it. But the assertive person knows he has the right to make mistakes without feeling guilty.

10. Blowing up at an employee is a hard-guy approach, showing no respect for the employee's rights and feelings. But (b) and (d) are nonassertive approaches to this problem. Figuring out what went wrong is the first step in an assertive approach.

11. It's normal to be a little nervous in this situation, but if you feel so uncomfortable that you can't even look the person in the eye, that's extreme nonassertiveness. If you can enjoy the interchange—great.

12. Managers who don't feel comfortable negotiating with subordinates sometimes make it a policy never to grant favors. The nice-guy manager just about always grants favors, and feels very uncomfortable if he doesn't. The assertive manager feels free to say "yes" or "no," depending on the circumstances.

How did you rate yourself on the assertiveness quiz? If you're like most people, you found yourself aggressive in some areas, assertive in others, and compliant in some. The authors' experience has been that a lack of assertive communication is responsible for most of the people troubles that occur on the job. We've also found that taking steps to improve the quality of communication can accomplish a great deal.

We feel that the underlying framework of assertiveness is a respect for others as well as for your own opinions, beliefs, and feelings. When we don't respect another person's feelings, we're likely act in an aggressive manner. If we don't respect our own, we tend to be compliant.

While most people probably wouldn't argue with this premise, it turns out that they often don't *act* on it. We've drawn below a few portraits of aggressive, compliant, and assertive types of managers. They are not portraits of real people, but they'll give you a feeling for the kinds of behavior characteristic of such types.

The Nice-Guy Manager

The nice-guy manager can't say "no" without feeling guilty. When the boss asks him or her to do something, he doesn't feel he has the right to refuse. When subordinates ask for a favor, he hates to refuse because he doesn't want to hurt them. His biggest worry is that people will judge him unfavorably.

This nice-guy, or compliant manager, does whatever he can to make people like him—he agrees with their opinions, laughs at their jokes (whether he gets them or not), and never rocks the boat. Chameleonlike, he blends into whatever group he's with.

He's likely to hesitate before he speaks, to talk softly, and to agree with others regardless of his own needs. He doesn't consider his own feelings to have any validity, and leaves it to those in "authority" to make the rules and judge him.

This manager would rather work 12 hours a day himself than face the difficulties of getting his subordinates to do their jobs properly. If he asks a subordinate to do something once, and they don't do it, he's likely to go and do it himself rather than ask again.

The compliant manager thinks negatively about himself and uses negative phrases. "This idea probably isn't worth anything, but . . ." "You're probably not interested in this, but . . ." When someone compliments his work, he's likely to shuffle his feet embarrassedly and mumble, "It really wasn't anything—the last part was pretty messed up—I should have done it better."

He is unable to negotiate a compromise with anyone because he at once gives in to the other person's demands. Therefore he prefers a highly structured en-

5

vironment in which everything is spelled out in neat little rules.

The biggest problem the nice-guy manager has is that he can't please everybody. How can he keep both upper management and his workers happy at the same time? His most anxious situation is when two people want different things from him.

The compliant manager feels powerless. He feels that other people are in charge of his life. He'll complain about "the company," "the boss," "the system" —anything but take responsibility for his own life.

The Tough-Guy Manager

The tough-guy manager believes in industrial psychologist McGregor's Theory X, which says that people are basically lazy, dishonest, stupid, and unwilling to work, and that you have to keep after them with a stick to get them to produce.

This manager approaches every conflict aggressively. He talks loudly and abusively, using gestures and eye contact aimed at bullying the other person into submissiveness.

The aggressive manager steps on the toes of anyone who gets in his way. He has no patience for weakness, and never allows himself to express any "soft" or "sensitive" feelings. He keeps his distance from people by building a protective wall around himself.

The Compliant/Aggressive Combination

An aggressive front often is used by people who are afraid to accept their own "weakness," or who have no confidence in their ability to negotiate for their rights. For example, by being hard-nosed all the time with their subordinates, they eliminate the need to relate to them as human beings.

Since the totally compliant person would have difficulty becoming a manager in the first place, what we often see is a manager who is compliant toward management above him, but aggressive toward his subordinates.

Whatever management says is good, wise, and sufficient. Whatever workers want must be bad—simply because they want it. This manager sees himself as a tool of the organization, taking orders from above and making sure they are carried out by the people below. He has a difficult time working with peers, because the lines of authority are not clearly drawn. Because he cannot communicate effectively and negotiate with peers, he detests "group work" and prefers to work alone.

The Assertive Manager

The assertive manager knows where he's going and has planned how to get there. But he's not rooted to old commitments. Instead, he updates his plans periodically and adjusts his goals to meet the changes in himself, in his opportunities, and in the world around him.

He has strong ideas and opinions, but he listens attentively to others—workers and management. He speaks frankly, and has a reputation for fairness and honesty.

He thinks well of himself, but he knows that he's not perfect and he will make mistakes. When he does, he admits it freely, without guilt. When others make mistakes, he focuses on correcting the error, not blaming.

The assertive manager knows himself well. He's aware of his strengths and weaknesses and does what he can to offset the weaknesses. But he doesn't apologize for them. He knows he's merely human—and that means imperfect by definition.

He's considerate of other people, but doesn't let himself be stepped on. He's not afraid to ask for what he wants, and to repeat himself if he's not heard the first time. When he doesn't get results one way, he tries another approach.

He gets along with his peers and works well in a group. He doesn't always try to get his way, but doesn't give in all the time, either. Able to distinguish the important issues from the unimportant, he knows when to fight and when to compromise.

Like anyone else, the assertive manager has fears,

but he makes himself act in spite of them when it's important. He takes risks, but not foolhardy ones. Before he makes a decision he calculates the odds realistically. But he makes decisions—and implements them with full commitment.

Being aware of his own weaknesses, he's aware that other people have them too. He tries to be understanding, but not self-sacrificing. He does what he can to help others cope, grow, and be responsible—but he doesn't carry their burdens, for he knows that they and they alone are responsible for their lives, just as he is responsible for his.

He's direct and forthright. People know that he means what he says. He stands erect, looks people in the eye when he talks to them, and appears at ease in any situation.

The assertive manager knows clearly what he wants to say before he says it. He considers whom he's talking to—and takes responsibility for what he says.

He doesn't take criticism personally. He deflects criticism that isn't important. If it is important, he tries to find out what the critic really means, and to learn from it if he can. Conflicts don't scare him.

He tells his subordinates what he expects from them. He gives them the tools they need to do their job—but allows them room for responsibility and growth. He's not threatened by them.

The assertive manager isn't afraid of expressing his feelings or needs. But he's aware of the appropriateness of a particular action. He doesn't act hastily, but considers the consequences first.

The assertive manager doesn't judge people by their race, skin color, sex, age, or religion. He realizes that different people have different styles and are entitled to their own opinions and beliefs. He knows there is more than one way to get a job done.

Where would you place yourself in the preceding descriptions? Probably you're a mixture: sometimes compliant, sometimes aggressive, sometimes assertive. The real questions to ask are: How effective a manager are you? And how do you feel about your behavior?

8

The goal of assertive communication is to help you accomplish what you want to, and to feel good about yourself while you're doing it. By accepting the fact that your feelings and needs are valid—and by getting that message across to others—you'll find your relationships with subordinates, peers, and superiors working better.

Many popular books on assertiveness think of the subject much more narrowly than we do. For us, it is a total communication process. A way of trying to be direct, to be open, to be clear, to say what we mean and want. And, on the other hand, to listen to others—to really hear their side of things, and to respect their feelings and opinions as valid. It also means respecting each person's way of dealing with the world: letting each one choose what is right for himself or herself, and in turn having the right to choose the way for ourselves.

The nice thing about assertive communication is that you can try it out in small steps. You can make a blunder and see what you're doing and learn from it. You can go back and patch things up. And you even can use your unassertiveness to help you *become* assertive.

Just being aware of your nonassertive behavior will help you change. And each time you behave in an assertive manner, you are likely to see results. That's the amazing thing about it—results are so easy to achieve.

The more we work in assertiveness training, the more we realize what a positive force we are dealing with. The more assertive people are, the better they feel about themselves. This in turn helps them to act more assertively. In addition, they present a model that encourages people around them to act assertively.

We're not saying this is a one-two-three magic formula for success and happiness. It isn't. But we have seen its results in our own lives and in the lives of many others, both on and off the job. **And you can get the same results.**

We're presenting the background and problems of nonassertive behavior in this chapter to show you the importance of assertive communication. This is like the "before" of before-and-after behavior. Don't let this negative side get you down. Help is on the way. "The Method" section of this book will show you concrete, easy-to-practice techniques for improving your own communication with peers, subordinates, and bosses.

Coping

One way to look at life is as a series of problems. If we feel we are able to cope, we see the problems as a challenge and welcome them. And each time we cope with one we feel stronger and better. But for the person who feels unable to handle the problems, life becomes overwhelming.

Management can be looked at in a similar way— as a series of challenges to be attempted with the best of our abilities and efforts.

But we have to accept the fact that not every step on this gameboard will be a forward move. We all make mistakes. Luck will sometimes go against us and affect us adversely. But no mistake need be final. As long as we are alive, there is *some* action we can take to try to improve our circumstances.

Goals

Most people are so busy just getting by from day to day that they don't have any feeling of progress. Things just happen. But the person who knows what he or she wants, and plans how to get it, will end up where he wants to be. If you don't plan, you drift.

The nonassertive person feels that he has no control, that everyone else gets to make the important decisions, that whatever he tries probably won't work anyway, so why bother? And he is right, for the nonassertive person pretty much lets other people run his life the way *they* want to.

Goal-setting is a way of taking control of your life. It involves deciding what you want now, next week, next year, in five years—and planning what steps to take to get there. But paper plans are useless unless there is an accompanying determination to carry them out.

The crisis-oriented management style aims at patching up things that go wrong, always just one jump ahead of disaster. Most of the manager's time and effort is spent fixing up what went wrong, correcting mistakes, plugging holes.

Some of this is necessary. There are times when everything will go wrong at once. You should always be prepared for Murphy's Law: "Everything that can possibly go wrong, will."

But a more effective management style is to analyze potential problems *before* they occur. To keep ahead of the crises as much as possible. And to plan positive steps as well.

Your department probably has goals that it's shooting for. But take a fresh look at your job. Free your mind. Imagine that you are starting in the position from scratch—creating your job—making it exactly what you think it should be.

How would you change it? What would you do to make your job utilize as many of your skills as possible? Or to make it a place where you can grow?

What do you need to work on in yourself? What skills, information, etc., do you need that you don't have now? What can you do to get them?

How do your job goals mesh with your personal goals? What's really important to you? Where do you want your career to take you? Be careful to choose goals based on what you *want*, not on what you think you *should* want.

The assertive person, instead of thinking of himself as a pawn of fate, management, the economy, or the government, realizes that even though the external world has an influence on his life, basically it's up to him. Sure, accidents happen, and luck "happens"— but if you look at people who are successful, generally they achieved what they set out to because they took charge of their own lives.

The thing to realize is that you have to keep pushing to get what you want. If you're pushed back three steps, keep going and try to move ahead four. If one path doesn't get you where you want to go, try another way. You may fail, but failures come to everybody. Failure is an opportunity to learn. Say to yourself, "O.K., what happened? What went wrong? What can I learn from this? How can it help me plan the next move?"

You have to take control. You can't let your subordinates push you from one end and your boss from the other; if you do, you won't be in control. Decide what you want to accomplish, based on the reality of what is possible out there.

What happens is largely up to you. There are all kinds of bosses with all kinds of personalities, problems, habits, and styles. Some are easy to work with, some hard. But very few of the bosses you will have will be impossible.

You'll find people who always complain, always jump from job to job looking for the perfect boss, the perfect setting, the perfect company, the perfect opportunity. Those people end up going nowhere. Because there is no perfect boss, or job, or company.

A friend of ours left the business world because he couldn't stand the office politics, the red tape, the hypocrisy. He had always dreamed of being a professor in a university, where people were concerned with important issues, and his ideas, talents, and brains would be valued. He got his wish; and when he became a professor, he found the bureaucracy, the politics, the pettiness worse than the things he had hated in the business world.

Yes, there are things to be put up with wherever you go. Life is not fair, and merit sometimes goes unrewarded. But if you're willing to persevere, the odds are workable.

Some people—managers and others—believe that the quality of employees' work has deteriorated in modern times and that this condition is irremediable. Some lay the blame on "the unions," and say that their hands are tied and that they are powerless to do anything about it except float along with the tide.

Such an attitude is defeatist, not assertive. It breeds ulcers and heart attacks. What should one do against obstacles? Instead of drifting with the tide, consider how a sailboat progresses: If you want to sail from

12

one point to another, and the wind is against you, you still can get where you want to go. By tacking—sailing at an angle to the wind instead of struggling directly against it and losing ground—you can reach your objective. The good sailor knows how to use the wind to get where he's going. You must try to be that good sailor, despite the obstacles. You mustn't beat your head against a wall in a doomed effort; instead, take a less direct approach where necessary. Work with—and within—the conditions that exist. Isn't it better to achieve a small gain than suffer a complete loss?

Taking Risks

Life is a precarious balance. We yearn for security, safety, warmth, and protection. But when these needs are satisfied, we become restless. We look for a challenge. We're ready to take a risk.

So we look beyond the safe arena we're in for something that will stretch our capacities—not to the point that they snap, but enough so that we grow and have the satisfaction of achievement, of overcoming our fear of failing to succeed.

This is the cycle: gathering strength; facing an obstacle; overcoming it; collapsing after the struggle; recouping our strength; and starting again. When we fail, it may take us longer to build up the strength to start again. But the cycle is repeated over and over again throughout our life.

Key factors in taking risks are the odds and the amount of the bet. The greater the stakes, the larger the chance of failure, the more you will sweat it out. And the bigger the thrill when you're successful.

Hiring a person, buying a piece of equipment, placing an ad—each decision can have negative consequences. Only by facing and accepting the possibility of failure can one make any decisions at all.

A series of decisions that turn out poorly can so weaken a person that he feels no longer able to make effective decisions. As he becomes more afraid of failure, the risk factor seems to escalate, and safety looms larger in importance. That's why it's important, after failure, to stop and recover one's strength; to sit down

13

and review what happened and why things went wrong; to assure oneself that one now has enough information to make a more knowledgeable decision the next time.

If you're not able to stand the maximum loss that may result from your action, don't make the bet. What this means is: If things don't turn out as you wish, can you accept and live with the worst possible consequences of your decision? To know the answer, you must first calculate what the consequences might be, and then think about them very hard, very dispassionately, very realistically.

Now, if you *can* accept those possible bad results, plan a contingency program: the steps you will take in the event of failure. Instead of a blind, unrealistic reliance on luck, you will then be prepared for almost anything.

This doesn't mean a lack of faith in your decision-making ability. Be optimistic. But be realistic: Know and accept the odds and the risk factor; know what you can do if things don't go as planned.

The manager who is prepared for the failures, who can switch gears in time because he or she is prepared —that is the truly successful manager. By blinding yourself to the possibility of failure, you may be thinking positively, but you also hamper yourself unnecessarily. People often will refuse to see that things are going wrong, and they then wait too long before taking action to cope with the situation. This is dangerous, for in the meantime the problem will have gotten worse, making it much harder to deal with.

COMMUNICATION: RISKS AND EXPECTATIONS

There are probably areas where you're very good at taking risks, or you wouldn't be a manager. But are you able to take risks in your everyday communication? Can you take the risk that someone won't like what you say—or will say "no" to your request?

Getting people to do things they may not like, asking questions that may elicit unpleasant answers, making requests that may be refused—all of this is part of your job as a manager.

A mother wrote to columnist Ann Landers complaining that her 18-year-old son never helped his father mow the lawn or shovel snow. She said they gave the boy a car to drive, gas, allowance, room, board, clothing, and love. But the father refused to ask or tell the boy to help. He thought the boy should see the need and do it without being asked.

This is a common mistake: expecting others to do what *we* think they *should* do. Sometimes people will meet your expectations and do things unasked, usually because they see things the same way you do. But if they don't, it's up to you to tell them what you want.

Some people try to avoid problems by saying nothing. Or else they wait too long to say something.

Instead of asking the boss for the raise they want, they silently wait it out, wanting to be spontaneously recognized for their excellence and merit. When Charlie the loudmouth gets a raise and they don't, they are righteously indignant. And they make themselves feel bad—unnecessarily.

Don't clam up and pout when people don't do what you secretly want them to. If you do, you're setting yourself up to be disappointed again and again, both in your managerial capacity and in your personal life. Instead, try assertive communication: let people know your wishes.

By contrast, the unassertive manager, instead of telling a new employee that he works too slowly, silently waits for the worker to improve. Then he waits longer—and still longer. After three months, he fires the man without warning, justifying the action to himself with: "He was slower than everyone else in the place, and I waited three months for him to speed up. I was more than fair."

By avoiding a problem and waiting for it to go away, the problem that initially was minor often escalates into something too big to handle smoothly, effectively, and with little pain. For example, by blinding himself to the necessity for controlling rapidly rising costs, a business manager may delay taking appropriate action—until finally he faces bankruptcy court.

15

Passive Aggression

This method often is used by people who feel powerless. When they cannot cope directly, they resist passively. Asked to do something they don't want to, they do it—but they make sure the job is loused up.

The passive aggressor feels put upon and used. He resents others telling him what to do. He resents the things he has to put up with each day. But instead of being direct, speaking up and asserting his rights, he expresses his resentment indirectly, performing the assignment inadequately or not finishing it on time.

The passive-aggressive worker may appear as a cooperative person who is simply a bungler. Whenever you ask him to do something, he readily agrees. But often it takes him longer than it should, or something goes wrong in the course of the job. He's not stupid or incompetent; he is merely expressing his resentment in the only way he feels is safe.

Unfortunately for the passive aggressor, this does him no good. He has to do the job over or take twice as long to get it done. Either way, his boss concludes that he is a poor worker. And he gets nowhere in more ways than one: Since no one can read his mind, they will continue to ask him to do the things he doesn't want to do.

Passive aggression is the way many people react to things that displease them: a smaller-than-expected raise, a supervisor's sharp tone of voice, an unfair division of overtime. Whatever it is that's bothering them, they say nothing about it. Instead, they find ways to "get back" by goofing off, making mistakes, breaking a tool.

This is one reason good communication lines are so important. If the worker can tell you what's on his mind and express his anger, chances are he won't have to use this underhanded approach. Try to tune in to the unspoken resentment in your people. Get them to express their feelings. Even if you can't change things or solve their problem every time, talking it over probably will dissipate their bad feelings so they won't have to engage in passive aggression.

Let's pause here for a moment's clarification. At

16

various times in the book we will caution you to respond only to the words the other person actually has spoken. Yet here we have just suggested that you listen for *un*spoken messages. How are you to know when each method is appropriate?

When you are feeling on the defensive or threatened, it's best to respond only to the other person's actual words. Don't try to read his or her mind or jump in to defend yourself against what you think he is about to say. Don't guess at the emotional content behind what you think is an attack. Instead, try to concentrate only on the actual words and respond only to what is actually said. If you are not sure what is meant, ask the person to clarify his statement.

But where you do not feel threatened and are not worried about defending yourself, try to listen beyond the words. Empathetically put yourself in the other person's place and imagine how you would feel if you were he. It's possible to do this only if you are relaxed and not worried about what the other person is thinking of you, or what your retort should be.

Are you a passive aggressor? How do you react when an executive decision is handed down that you don't like? Or when your boss does something that you think is unfair? Perhaps you don't consciously drag your feet when things aren't going your way. Maybe you say to yourself, "That's the way it is; I'll just have to swallow it."

You may think you're swallowing it—but your resentment may show without your being aware of it. Do "things" often go wrong—just as you predicted— after an executive decision you didn't agree with? The next time you're in this situation, observe yourself and see if you are able to note any signs of passive aggression. It's not an effective way of coping, so you're only hurting yourself in the long run.

What can you do about it if you *are* passively aggressing? Becoming aware of it will help. Secondly, you can make sure you've done your best to communicate your viewpoint to those in higher management. Have you presented them with an alternative plan to the one they intend to use? Have you made a solid case for your raise (or whatever it is you want)?

17

Once you've presented your case in an assertive and thorough manner, you should feel better about it, even if you lose. What more can you do than your best? Furthermore, not even you will always be right!

Be Assertive

Passive aggression, avoidance, and other attempts to eliminate risk-taking don't work. So you may as well stand up, say your piece, and do your thing.

"What if I fail?"

That is the crux of risk-taking: the "what-if." Well, you're perfectly right. You may fail. You may lose. But you also may win.

By and large, the ones who have made it in this world are those who tried and failed—and tried again. And you can bet that the guy—or gal—who doesn't try at all never gets off first base.

Of course you know this. The difficulty is acting on it, and doing so in everything you do. Sometimes the toughest things are the little ones—like asking a peer not to smoke while you're eating lunch, or asking your secretary to make wider margins on letters.

Like most people, you probably find that it's easy to be assertive in some areas, and difficult in others. Observe yourself for a few days and note what kinds of situations make you hesitant about speaking your piece. What kinds of aggravations do you submit to day after day, rather than face a confrontation?

Once you've decided what areas need work, you can take steps to systematically handle them more assertively. The chapters that follow will give you the specific techniques to do the job.

The Method

THE ELEMENTS

Work on Your Self-Image

Negative action is usually caused by negative thinking. By thinking well of yourself, you'll encourage others to think well of you. By believing you are capable of accomplishing something, you'll be able to do it.

If you have a poor self-image, there are any number of factors that might have contributed to it. As children, most of us were told not to brag about our accomplishments. Humility was rewarded, and we were encouraged not to think of ourselves as better than anyone else.

So much stress has been put on this type of attitude that many people think less of themselves than they should. We don't suggest that you go to the other extreme and become a self-satisfied egotist. But we believe you might benefit from a re-evaluation, with emphasis on your strengths and accomplishments. The questions and exercises that follow will help you do this.

If you were your boss, how would you describe yourself to a stranger?

How do you think your subordinates and co-workers would rate you?

Now, how about your own self-rating:

List your five worst qualities below, or on a separate sheet of paper.

_____
_____
_____

List your five best qualities.

_____
_____
_____
_____
_____

Did you have more trouble with the best qualities than with the worst? If so, you may have a weak self-image.

Most of us have spent our lives waiting for other people to compliment us. From the time we were little kids, we beamed when Mom or Dad praised us for getting an *A*, catching a ball, etc. We're still doing things in order to have others tell us we're good, clever, or talented.

It's time to start praising yourself instead of waiting for other people to do it. Forget that old idea that you should be humble. Stop putting yourself down. Stop trying to live up to other people's ideas of what is good, right, and worth attaining.

You're only as good as you think you are. With a low self-image, how do you expect anyone else to think well of you? A poor self-image leads to pessimism, fear of failure, loss of interest in life.

You are an important person. You have things to contribute that no one else has. Stop dwelling on the minuses; start patting yourself on the back for the pluses.

IMAGE-BUILDER EXERCISES

1. List ten things you do very well:

_____
_____
_____

20

_____

_____

_____

_____

_____

_____

2. List five ideas you have contributed to help your company save money, time, materials, etc.:

_____

_____

_____

_____

_____

3. First thing in the morning, every day, think of one thing that you accomplished the previous day. Write it down.

Let the World Know How Good You Are

People like to be winners. Make your subordinates and yourself feel that you're all part of a winning team by blowing your own horn. Tell your boss and co-workers about your department's accomplishments: how a rush order was gotten out, how a tough problem was solved, etc.

Tell them at coffee break and lunch. Tell them in memos and reports. People will believe what you tell them—if you do it tactfully, with facts to back it up. It will give your people a real boost, too, to know that you're proud of them and their accomplishments.

When someone compliments you, accept it graciously. It's a typical trait of the nonassertive manager to reply to a compliment: "It was just part of the job," or, "It wasn't anything."

When someone compliments you or your department, say "THANK YOU," or, "YES, WE REALLY WORKED HARD TO ACCOMPLISH IT," or whatever is appropriate.

In numerous observations in our assertiveness work of people talking together, one of the prime findings is how easy it is for people to misunderstand each other. Words dart and flow, back and forth—but they often miss their targets. So this book includes much important information on communication, because assertiveness *is* communication: There's no such thing as being assertive if you aren't getting your message through.

And the opposite is also true: Fouling up the communication lines is being nonassertive. For example, if you say things so that people don't understand what you mean, that may provide a perfect excuse for you to say, "No one ever does what I ask them to."

Words

One of the basic obstacles to effective communication is the medium we use: words. When we want to talk about a chair or a typewriter, we use a word that signifies *chair* or *typewriter*. This isn't so bad, since most people are capable of connecting the abstract to the concrete.

But what about words like "efficient" and "loyal"? You can't really point to an "efficient" or a "loyal," can you? So now we come to a necessary basic for communication: agreement on the meanings of words.

You may say this is a simple matter of getting out the dictionary. But that would only slow things down and result in tedious arguments. Besides, the real "meaning" that words have for us is made up of the countless numbers of associations we've had with that word—every sentence we've read or heard it in.

> "We learn the meanings of practically all our words, not from dictionaries, not from definitions, but from hearing these noises as they accompany actual situations in life and then learning to associate certain noises with certain situations."*

* Hayakawa, S.I. *Language in Thought and Action.* Harcourt Brace & World, Inc., 1939.

Luckily, most people agree enough about a basic core of words so that they *can* talk to each other. But because there are differences, no matter how slight, in the meanings people ascribe to words, it's necessary to make sure the other person really gets the message clearly. How can that be done?

Reinforcement. Verbal communication is one of the modes of expression available to us. But there are others. And one way to help your message get through is to reinforce it by saying the same thing in these different modes. For example, when you say that you are pleased with something, you'll probably have a pleased expression, or perhaps be smiling. Your facial expression, bodily gestures, and tone of voice all complement the message you're sending.

Sometimes a simple repetition of an idea will help the other person remember your message. For example, if early in the day you tell your secretary that you will be attending a meeting from lunch until three o'clock, when you leave for lunch you could remind her that you will be back from the meeting at three.

Of course, one can also reinforce negative messages in several ways. Verbally, for example: "I thought you'd have that done by now! Gee, I'm disappointed in you. How come you didn't get it finished? Now everyone's going to be held up because of you!"

Another way to reinforce a spoken message is with a confirming written message, such as a memo or letter. You might use this method when you've gotten a favorable response to a presentation at a meeting. Write a memo summing up what happened and the steps to be taken next.

Speak in Specifics, Not in Generalities. Another roadblock to understanding is the use of vague, abstract, general words instead of specific, concrete ones. The more generalized your message, the more room there is for differing interpretations.

To avoid misunderstandings, always use the most precise, specific word you can. Where possible, use numbers and names to pinpoint exactly what you mean. Look at these examples:

GENERAL	SPECIFIC
"We've got to get moving."	"Everyone in the department must increase his production by 5 percent."
"Put it there."	"Put the package on the floor next to the back wall."
"I'd like to know I'm appreciated around here."	"I want a $5,000 raise."
"I'd like delivery as soon as possible."	"The order must be in our warehouse by November 15th."
"Some people have been abusing their privileges around here."	"Sandra, Carl, and Eric have been taking two-hour lunches every day this week."

Context. The context, or situation in which the message is given, influences the results of the communication. Is it the president of the company talking, or one of your co-workers? Are you at lunch, or in the conference room? Have you just submitted a report, been given a raise, or made a costly error? Are you standing or sitting? Is the other person smiling or frowning?

When you talk to your subordinates, be sure the context is appropriate. If you want them to feel relaxed, for example, don't call them into your office and let them stand for 15 minutes while you negotiate big deals on the phone.

If you want someone's full attention, *don't* pick a moment when he's in the middle of an intricate operation to speak to him. And be careful that your tone, pitch, and gestures match the meaning you want to convey. A lot of people are amazingly sensitive to such nonverbal clues. If they read you as angry, they won't believe you when you say you're not.

If someone goes out and buys Zippo soap after reading an advertisement in a magazine, the ad was effective. Finding out that the ad sold a lot of soap gives the ad writer the feedback that his message got through. This kind of feedback may not come for many weeks.

But there are times when you would rather not wait to see results in order to find out if a message got through. When you give instructions to an employee you don't think: "It'll be interesting to see if he does what I told him to or screws up the job."

Feedback. If you take a conversational course in French, you can get feedback on how well you did in various ways. You can take an exam and see how well you answered the questions. Or you can go to Paris and talk to people and see if you understand each other.

In communication, feedback is something that lets you know whether the other person got your message. Did he understand what you said? Did he believe what you said? Did he do what you said?

One of the simplest ways to get feedback is to ask the listener to tell you what you said:

"Would you mind repeating back my instructions? I just want to make sure we're in agreement."

Don't say, "Did you understand what I said?" Most people will automatically say "yes" to questions like that. Instead, get them to rephrase what you said in their own words. Otherwise they can parrot back your words without the vaguest notion of what you're talking about.

Asking for feedback is a simple tool that should be used much more often than it is. We'll agree it's not feasible to use it all the time: You can't very well finish every conversation with your boss by saying, "Now would you repeat back to me what I just said so I can be sure you're not off in left field somewhere?"

But you can get feedback by summing up what was said in a conversation and asking the other person to agree that this is indeed what the two of you have been talking about:

"Then you agree that we should . . ."
"Then I can go ahead with my plan to . . ."

25

"Let me go over the details once more to be sure we agree."

Good intentions deserve good execution. Poor feedback may be worse than none at all. For example:

Jim asks his secretary to call Ken, a new employee, into his office. Ken comes immediately to Jim's office, but Jim is on the phone. Ken waits outside for 10 minutes, becoming more and more nervous as he ponders the possible reason for this meeting.

Jim finishes his phone call and calls Ken in. But Jim immediately gets another phone call, which he takes before asking Ken to sit down. Ken stands until Jim finishes the call. Jim asks him to sit down.

Still frowning because of the message he received in the last phone call, Jim says to Ken: "Just wanted to let you know you're doing O.K., Ken, but you need to get out in the field more."

At that point Jim's secretary walks in and gives him a message. Jim stands up and says to Ken: "I'm sorry I don't have more time now. We'll have a longer chat another time, O.K.?" Ken answers "Sure," and leaves.

What is the message Ken gets from this interchange? The boss was frowning when he spoke to him. The boss said Ken needed more field work—Ken wasn't sure what that meant. Now Ken is puzzled, discouraged, and anxious.

Jim *wanted* to let Ken know that he was coming along fine in the job and was ready to start accompanying the field representatives. But he let the context become one where Ken was ill at ease and expected bad news.

Jim's frown conflicted with the brief message that Ken was doing O.K., so Ken missed that part of the message completely. Jim should have elaborated on this point and expressed it more emphatically with appropriate facial and bodily gestures.

The third part of the message—about the field work—was too general. Ken had no idea what Jim meant by it.

Also, Jim let the exchange end without getting any feedback from Ken, which meant Jim had no idea how his message was received. All in all, it was a flop.

Because no two people have exactly the same experience, accurate communication is difficult. And if we can't express our needs and wants to others so that they understand the message, how can we expect to get what we ask for?

Part of assertiveness is using the tools of effective communication, making sure our messages are clear and that we truly have been understood.

An unassertive person makes a few half-hearted attempts and gives up. He—or she—doesn't take the pains to give a clear message because he's not sure he has a right to ask. He's afraid his message isn't worth getting across.

Some people put the blame on others. They expect the listener to take the responsibility for hearing them correctly. But to get the results you desire, recognize that it is *your responsibility to make sure people hear you.*

Make Sure People Hear You

1. Use words that they are likely to understand and relate to.
2. Give your message in more than one way. Use gestures, tone of voice, and facial expressions to emphasize your meaning.
3. Don't speak in generalities and abstract terms.
4. Be specific. Use names of things ("the package," "the back wall"), names of people, and numbers where possible.
5. Make sure the context fits, not fights, the message.
6. Try to talk to people when they are likely to be in a receptive frame of mind.
7. Don't assume the person understood your message.
8. Get feedback, either in words ("You want this sent first class mail, then?") or actions (watch an employee operate a machine for several minutes to make sure he understands your instructions).

Listening. Talking is only half the communication process. Listening is the other half. If we don't listen well, we probably won't talk effectively, either. But good listening doesn't come easily.

People think much faster than they talk; when someone is talking to you, therefore, your mind has time to wander. There's a tendency to think you know what the person is saying half-way through his sentence, to draw conclusions before he finishes his statement—even to start forming your rebuttal before he has finished speaking.

It takes special effort to be a good listener. You must attentively concentrate on the speaker's words, gestures, tone: Who is he and why is he saying this? How does he feel about what he's saying? What is the intent of his message? What is he trying to get me to do or feel or say? What does he mean—not the literal meaning of his words, but the meaning behind them?

Open and Closed Minds. Milton Rokeach of Michigan State University * points out that there are four possible ways in which a listener can react to a speaker:

1. Accept the speaker and accept his statement;
2. Accept the speaker but reject his statement;
3. Reject the speaker but accept his statement;
4. Reject the speaker and reject his statement.

The person with a closed mind is able to have only reactions 1 and 4. He has to accept or reject both speaker *and* statement. His mind is not open to the more moderate positions.

When you work with people day in and day out, there's a tendency to classify them as types, to put them in boxes: Helen is highly competent; Jack always exaggerates; Ken is a complainer.

When people first meet someone, they are usually open-minded (unless they've been prepped beforehand on what to expect). They wait to see what the new person's style is. Each subsequent interaction with the person gives new information for the box: "That's the second time Jerry was late on an assignment. He's probably one of those guys who can't meet deadlines."

* Rokeach, Milton. *The Open and Closed Mind.* Michigan State University, 1960.

28

The boxes are O.K. as long as they're continually updated in accord with new information. The problem occurs when people form the box quickly, and then keep it static no matter what the person says or does in the future. When the person says something that doesn't fit his or her box, these people think: "That's not like Harry—he must be out of sorts today."

How often do you react to what you expect a person to say rather than to what he is actually saying? That's because of the box you've put him in.

Very often people are thrown into boxes without saying a word. They are pegged as a certain type because they are manager or worker; from accounting or production; male or female; black or white; old or young. This stereotyping leaves little room to hear what the person is actually saying.

Making Judgments. It's necessary to make value judgments in order to get along in this world. At some point you have to decide if a particular supplier has a better piece of equipment for your needs than another supplier; if an employee will work out or not; if a particular plan should be adopted.

As long as you make value judgments appropriately —that is, with adequate information—and as long as you're willing to change your mind if new evidence is presented, all is well. But jumping to conclusions and sticking permanent labels on people, ideas, and things is not the sign of a thinking manager.

The worst way to make judgments is on hearsay:

When Ella is transferred to another department, her old boss tells Phil, the new one, that Ella is a slow worker. So Phil assumes he'll have the same problem with her. Perhaps he gives Ella a pep talk about quotas—tells her she can't goof off here like she did in Joe's department.

Now Ella thinks to herself, "This new guy's a son-of-a-bitch just like Joe. He doesn't even give me a chance. I'll be damned if I'm going to put myself out for him!"

Another result of premature judging is that it often

evokes from people the behavior you expect. The act of labeling people seems to carry with it a great deal of the self-fulfilling-prophecy phenomenon.

Making premature judgments—especially based on other people's negative conclusions—hinders assertive communication. When a friend of ours joined a company, he decided to propose a new way of doing a particular project. His colleagues tried to dissuade him from suggesting it, for others had tried to make this change in the past and had been turned down. But our friend went ahead with his plan. He developed the most thoughtful, positive proposal he could—and the boss accepted it.

We don't advocate that you ignore clues from your own and others' experiences. But don't be too quick to give up on a person or project just because others have. Treat bosses as if they were competent, fair, and interested in implementing good ideas. Treat employees as if they were honest, bright, and interested in doing a good day's work. Only when the *facts* tell you otherwise—facts based on your own observations—should you alter your judgment.

When collecting facts on which to base judgments, try to get them first hand. Other people's "facts" often are distorted. And get specific details whenever possible. "John is lazy" is somebody's conclusion; "John failed to complete six assignments" is specific, and because it reports an objective, ascertainable fact, it is the kind of statement that is less apt to reflect bias.

Find out reasons for things. For example, if someone comes to work late, don't assume that person is lazy or uncaring. Find out *why* he was late. Note how many times it occurs. Explain to him why it's important not to be late, and tell him you expect him to make every effort to come in on time. Give him a reasonable period of time to change his habits.

If things don't improve after you've explained the consequences of coming in late, then you can be pretty accurate when you say: "It appears from the evidence that Charles is not going to come in on time." (Note that you still haven't made a judgment as to *why,* such as, "He's irresponsible," or "He's looking to be fired.")

Making judgments that are as accurate as possible,

based on relevant facts, is an important aspect of the management job. Timing of decisions is also vital. To postpone judgments past the point when they should be made can be dangerous. Procrastination because you're afraid you don't have *all* the facts can lead to your being unable to make any decisions because you're afraid they might be wrong. Anybody who is a doer will make some mistakes. That's part and parcel of being human.

Empathy. The way to really hear another person is through empathy. Put yourself mentally into that person's mind. Make yourself aware of his or her feelings, his or her point of view.

Don't spend your listening time thinking up counter-arguments—which means you are rejecting what he is saying—but instead suspend your own point of view for the moment and put yourself in his shoes.

The best way to be sure you've heard another person accurately is to repeat back to him what he said, in your own words:

"You mean you feel you've been getting most of the dirty jobs around here lately?"

When you can state the other person's point of view to his satisfaction, you've heard him. Very often, he will refine your statement further:

"I don't mean just me. Jerry and Lewis get them a lot, too . . . but a lot of the guys never get their hands dirty. I think the messy stuff should be distributed more equitably among everybody."

This kind of empathic listening, where you repeat back to the person what he said, is sometimes called "nondirective listening." It's nondirective because you're not channeling—directing—the other person's thoughts in any particular direction. That's why it's an excellent way of helping people get things off *their* chest, instead of asserting yourself into the picture. And it helps you understand what's really on their mind. This method is used in many counseling situations.

31

Here's an example of it in a work situation: Phyllis's secretary, Sharon, walks into Phyllis's office and says in an emotionally upset tone: "I'm so angry, I could cry!"

PHYLLIS	I can see you *are* angry.
SHARON	That Bernice makes me *so* mad!
PHYLLIS	Bernice has made you angry?
SHARON	Yes! No matter what the typing pool is doing for anyone else, Bernice tells them *her* work has priority!
PHYLLIS	You're upset because she's putting her work before yours?
SHARON	Right. The report that should have been finished this morning isn't done because Bernice gave them other work to do first! Now the report's going to be late!
PHYLLIS	You're worried about the report being late.
SHARON	Oh, luckily they'll be able to have it done by early afternoon, anyway. But what gripes me is that this happens all the time!
PHYLLIS	This has happened to you before?
SHARON	Yes! Bernice thinks her work is so important, she always puts it before mine! And those girls in the typing pool do whatever she says! No one listens to me!
PHYLLIS	You're upset because the girls in the typing pool listen to Bernice, not you.
SHARON	Oh, I guess it's not their fault. They just take orders. Bernice is the one I have the argument with. I've got to get her to stop doing this to me.
PHYLLIS	So your problem is with Bernice.
SHARON	Yes, I guess I just have to have it out with her.
PHYLLIS	You're worried about a confrontation?
SHARON	Yes, I hate them. But if I don't do something, this is just going to happen again and again.

32

PHYLLIS	So even though you don't like to do it, you're going to have to talk to her?
SHARON	I guess so.

By the end of this conversation Sharon is considerably calmer and ready to face her problem rationally. Note that Phyllis never once suggested what Sharon should do about her problem. She simply restated what Sharon told her each time, focusing on the feelings Sharon had about the situation.

In addition to helping people dissipate hurt and angry feelings, this is an excellent way to encourage them to solve their own problems. It may be difficult at first to resist giving them a solution, especially if you think one is obvious. But telling people what to do doesn't help them develop their own problem-solving skills.

Many times people are not looking for solutions when they complain about things. They simply want to complain and are seeking a sympathetic ear. In such cases you will simply irritate them by trying to solve their problems. For example:

Co-workers Stan and Phil are having lunch together:

STAN	Boy, they gave us *some* production quota this week! I don't know how we're going to make it.
PHIL	Why don't you tell Harry about it?
STAN	Nah . . . he won't do anything. He's too worried about his image with the big brass!
PHIL	What about getting some extra help?
STAN	Wouldn't be worth it—it would take too much time to split up the work and break them in.
PHIL	How about overtime?
STAN	Everybody's working the limit now. I can't ask them to do any more, they'll all up and quit!
PHIL	It looks like you'll just have to get them to knuckle under and work faster.

33

STAN   I'm sick and tired of having to ask my men to do that! What does Harry think we're made of, anyway?

Instead of dissipating Stan's anger, Phil's problem-solving approach served to make Stan even more enraged. Stan didn't want Phil to solve his problem; he wanted a sympathetic ear to bitch to. Besides, Stan had probably already considered the alternatives mentioned by Phil, and knew he was left with no choice but getting his men to knuckle under.

There was no way Phil could solve Stan's problem. But he might have helped him get a load off his chest by nondirective listening—listening without telling him what he should do.

Contrary to a common misconception, it is not assertive to give people advice when they haven't asked for it. Frequently it is a sign of the opposite of assertiveness: For example, when somebody complains about something, a compliant person's sense of inadequacy may cause a vague feeling of guilt, as though her or she were responsible for the trouble and had to cure it.

The aggressive person, on the other hand, assumes that he or she knows what is right for everyone else. If other people would simply take his advice, they'd easily solve their problems. If they aren't interested in his advice, or don't follow it, they are stupid and destined to failure.

Be extremely wary of giving people advice. When it's not asked for, *never* give it. Even when people ask for advice, they often don't want it. And even when they *do* want it, you probably will be better off helping them think through to their own solution than giving them one ready-made by you:

Jerry approaches his sales manager with a problem:

JERRY   Frank, I've got a problem I don't know how to handle.

FRANK   What is it?

JERRY   I promised Penco delivery on their

34

	order two weeks from today. But just now Ed told me there's no way we can do it.
FRANK	You're trying to find a way to get the order out in spite of what Ed said?
JERRY	No, there's no way to do that. I'm trying to figure out what to say to Penco. I shouldn't have promised the two-week delivery until I checked with Ed. Now I'm in a fix.
FRANK	You made a promise you couldn't keep.
JERRY	Yeah, I really wanted the order, and I knew they had to have the stuff right away. If I didn't promise two-week delivery they would have bought from XCo instead of us.
FRANK	Then without the two-week delivery, there's no order?
JERRY	That's right. That means my only alternative is to figure out *some* way to get it to them in two weeks—or give up the order.
FRANK	So if you want the order, you've got to deliver the goods quickly.
JERRY	Right. I wonder if there's a way to exchange part of MCo's shipment that's going out the end of this week. They ordered the same stock numbers . . . if I talk to Jim, maybe he could work something out . . .
FRANK	It sounds like a decent possibility.
JERRY	Yeah, I'd better get to Jim right away. Thanks for the help, Frank!

Frank could have saved time and told Jerry immediately to find a similar shipment going out sooner and exchange some of the stock, and that would have solved Jerry's present dilemma. But it wouldn't help him develop his problem-solving ability. He would become more dependent on Frank's advice.

Mind Reading. Because people think faster than someone can talk, and because they're always trying to save time, they read the person's mind instead of listening to what he has to say.

At the next social event you attend, observe how many times people have their sentences finished by others. Husbands and wives are especially apt to indulge in this habit.

Sometimes people finish somebody else's sentence because it's important to them to "prove" they understand what he means. But even if they *can* finish his sentence adequately, he won't like it.

If you finish the sentence of an aggressive person, he's likely to tell you off: "Will you shut up until I finish?" Compliant people, on the other hand, may let you go ahead *even if what you say is not what they meant!* They are so unassertive that they won't contradict you even if you turn their sentence into something entirely different from what they intended. In dealing with such a person you must be especially careful that you don't finish his sentences, or you may never find out what he really meant to say.

Sometimes unassertive people will finish another's sentences as a way of proving that they know what's going on, that they not only *understand* the other's point of view but even feel the same way. This is a reflection of their need to be accepted and liked by everyone.

Sometimes mind-readers block out not only ends of sentences, but whole conversations. They don't bother to finish the sentence or interrupt; they sit there as if they are listening, but their minds have floated off into space. They assume they know what the speaker was going to say anyway—so why bother listening? The time could be better spent figuring out what they themselves—the more important speaker (in their eyes)—will say next. Of course, their remarks often are totally inappropriate because they were wrong in their mind reading.

Expecting Other People to Read Your Mind. This is the other side of the mind-reading coin. You say to yourself: "They know how I feel." Of course. Your subordinate should *know* that sloppiness aggravates you. Your boss should *know* that you're ready for more responsibility. Your co-worker should *know* that you can't afford to take two-hour lunches the way he can.

There really is no way for people to read your mind. Yet people depend on it to an amazing degree. They will let an annoying situation go on and on, assuming the other party knows it's bothering them. They won't simply speak up and say what's on their mind.

This attitude is a natural for the unassertive person. It's a way to feel sorry for yourself without ever having to take responsibility for your plight. After all, if people know what hurts you, and they do it anyhow, then it's *their* fault, not yours. You can go around with your head in the sand, feeling very angry, and thinking the whole world has it in for you.

It's also a kind of passive aggression not to tell people when they're doing something that's bothering you. Or not to ask for what you want. Because while you're not complaining, your hostility is building up. You'll find other ways to get back at them.

One way is to make them feel guilty. For example, subtly mention the fact that they have been annoying you (neglecting you, etc.) with their behavior for the past three years. But you, a morally superior person, have borne the brunt of this mistreatment without complaint. Now don't they feel guilty!?

"Oh, you gave that empty office to Carolyn? I've been hoping and waiting to get into an office that size for the last five years!"

"Yes, my cough is getting worse. I'm going for lung tests next week. Your cigar? No, don't put it out. If I could put up with it all these years, there's no point in your stopping now."

"They just took Ron to the hospital. What else has to happen before you'll stop leaving boxes in the aisles where people can break their necks on them?"

Expecting others to read our minds and know what we want is a very common fault. It is a powerful weapon—and it usually is self-employed against oneself. The next time you feel that someone is doing

37

something *in order to* hurt you, stop and think. Are you absolutely sure they know your preferences in the matter at hand? Have you *told* them—clearly—how you feel about it? Or have you assumed that they know that anybody would feel the way you do? And even if you have told them, they probably have forgotten. It is relatively rare that somebody acts for spite; usually they are merely doing what comes naturally to them, what they've done all their lives, for their own reasons, which have nothing to do with you. Think about it—aren't we all like that?

To Listen Effectively:

1. Focus on the actual words, gestures, and tone of the speaker.
2. Try not to have a preconceived notion of what the speaker will say, or what point of view he might have. In other words, keep your mind open.
3. Don't extend what people say to a conclusion *you* think should naturally follow. Respond to what *they* actually say. For example, if your boss asks you when a report will be ready, simply answer his question. Don't assume he is complaining about it not being done now. If you're not sure about someone's intent—ask. Don't assume something negative and get defensive.
4. Don't jump to conclusions about people without adequate facts. Keep revising your picture of people as you get new information.
5. Judge people's *actions* rather than stereotyping the *person:* "John has had three accidents this month," not "John is a careless, clumsy bungler."
6. Expect the best from people.
7. To understand people when they talk to you, put yourself in their shoes. Try to imagine how they are thinking and feeling.
8. When people are upset about something, or have a problem, try helping them with nondirective listening: Repeat back to them, in your own words, what they have just said, emphasizing their *feelings* about the problem: "You feel that you're getting a raw deal."

Don't argue with them, or defend yourself, or point out how they're being illogical, or try to give them solutions to their problem.

Do as little of the talking yourself as possible. Give the other person plenty of room to open up.

9. Don't read people's minds. Let them finish their own sentences.
10. Don't spend listening time thinking of what you're going to say next. *Listen.*
11. Don't expect other people to read *your* mind. *Tell* them what you want.
12. Check *yourself* out. Do you have trouble "hearing" people?

Do you want so much to prove to people that you're "with" them that you finish their sentences or nod your head before they've had their say? Do you miss what is said because you're busy thinking worrisome thoughts about something you may have done, or wondering what the speaker is thinking of you?

These things may be signs of unassertiveness. Not being sure of yourself, you are unable to really listen to the other person. As you become more confident and relaxed, this won't happen as much. But you may have gotten into bad habits that are hard to shake. Observe yourself next time you're in such a situation; consciously try to forget yourself and empathize with the speaker. Don't finish anyone else's sentence. Make yourself pause and think before you answer, particularly with stressful questions. It's O.K. to pause to think, to consider, to reflect—instead of blurting out an answer. In fact, people will think more of you for it, not less. You don't have to have instantaneous answers to everything.

And don't be impulsive when you're asked a question. Many questions are rhetorical; i.e., the speaker doesn't expect an answer. A student of ours told us how she had taken a seat in the vice president's office one day to discuss something. He pointed to his name-plate facing her on the desk and said, "Do you know why I have this here?" Instead of giving the natural answer—"No, why?"—she immediately jumped to a guilty conclusion and said, "Because I spelled your name wrong?"

Why did he have his nameplate there? Because it hid a transistor radio—he liked to play music while he worked. In other words, while he was just making friendly small talk, revealing a bit of himself, she assumed she had to give an answer—and she automatically picked a self-reproaching one.

Talking

Managers often spend a great deal of effort trying to write better letters and memos, develop better training programs, and improve meetings and conferences. But they very often neglect the most common form of communication: the talking that goes on every day with superiors, peers, and subordinates. Yet this is the level on which many misunderstandings occur.

Consider Your Listener. The first step in effective talking is to get the person's attention. Is your listener listening to you? Or is a machine buzzing nearby? Or is he momentarily occupied with a pleasant daydream?

There's no point in beginning your message until you have the person's attention. Make your first words do this job and no other: "Harry, I'd like to talk to you for a minute."

One of the best ways to get someone to listen to what you're saying is to point out how they will benefit. If your message is about something that will make a worker's job easier, save your boss money, or increase a co-worker's productivity, let them know in the beginning: "I'd like to talk to you about an idea I have that might cut costs in the shipping department."

Use words and phrases that are appropriate to the listener. For example, don't use technical terms with a customer who won't understand them. And don't *over*-simplify when talking to an "expert" who will be insulted by it.

We don't mean you should mimic the talk of people around you. Don't try to be "one of the guys" in the plant and a cultured snob in the executive suite. Be yourself. Use language that you're comfortable with. But modify your language to fit the context. Listen to yourself for a few days to see if you use too many difficult or technical words, complex sentences, etc., that may make it tough for people to understand you.

When considering your listener, remember that he may have a preconceived notion of your motives. For example, some workers are always suspicious of "management." If they are on guard, ready to defend, they may hear only what they expect to hear, and your actual words will go right past them. Until they are confident that you are leveling with them, you may have to make an extra effort to get them to *hear* you.

Be aware of the pressures on people. "People under tension, anxious, unsure of themselves, are likely to call names, show prejudice, impugn motives, get angry, and generally scramble communication lines." *

Before you begin talking to someone, put yourself in his or her shoes. How is he feeling? What are his interests in the matter you're discussing? What kind of a base do the two of you have—things you can agree on to begin with?

Be careful not to use words that will irritate your listener. Once you've angered him, there's no way he can listen objectively to the rest of what you want to tell him.

Logic and Reason. People don't usually act on logic and reason. They act on feelings, opinions, and beliefs. There's nothing wrong with that. Actually, our western culture has at times put too much emphasis on logical reasoning, especially the two-valued logic of right and wrong. Reality is complex, and there often are far more than two sides to a question.

Logic is fine when you know all the variables. But in real life there are many variables we cannot be sure of. Add to that the individual emotional needs and wants of the people involved, and you have a situation in which you can't convince people through logic.

Consider, as an example, the use of laetrile in treating cancer. "Reasonable" people might say it should be outlawed because it has been proven to be ineffective.

* Chase, Stuart. *Power of Words*. Harcourt Brace & Co., 1953.

41

We're in a fix to begin with. What does this proof consist of? Who has tried it, and in how many cases? Who conducted the experiments? Which experts should we listen to? What percentage of cures must be obtained in order to say it "works"? And what about the fact that placebos—sugar pills—have "cured" people of all kinds of things?

In writing these paragraphs, we aren't taking a position for or against the legalization of laetrile. We're simply illustrating how difficult it is to solve everything with logic and reason.

Some people act as if the fact that their argument is logical means everyone must accept it. (This approach *will* bulldoze some people—especially compliant people who feel they have no right to argue with logic—into accepting what they say as truth.) If you have expected people to bow to your finer reasoning in the past, maybe it's time to try a new tack. Perhaps if you appealed to people's self-interest, or other feelings and beliefs, you might have a better chance of convincing them.

After all, a rational approach to life is one that considers all variables. People who push logic or rationality often are simply pushing their own brand of reasoning. A true rationality considers the emotions and other "illogical" input—even if irrational—because these factors matter: They are influential; they move people.

A variation of the logic approach is the "rules" approach. You expect people to do what you say because "it's company policy" or "it's in the rulebook." Some people will go along—at least while you're watching. But they'll be much more cooperative if you can point out *why* it's company policy, or *why* it's a rule, and show them the benefit.

Take traffic laws, for example. Some people will obey them no matter what. They could be sitting at a red light at 4 o'clock in the morning with no cars in sight—and sit there until it turns green. Other people will take a careful look around, make sure no cops are in sight, and go on through.

Generally, nonassertive people do not question rules. Before doing anything different, they always want to know if it is against the law or company policy. They don't ask if it is a useful action, but if it is a legal action: "Are we allowed to do that?"

Sometimes companies have arbitrary rules that irritate employees without serving any useful purpose. For example, take employee lunch hours. It *may* make the operation run smoother if everyone takes the same lunch hour. But in many cases it wouldn't matter if a worker took his or her lunch hour at a different time.

If you must have people follow rules such as these, at least let them know *why*. But if possible, give them freedom to make their own decisions in these areas. They will appreciate the fact that you consider them human beings, not machines.

People's feelings are important, no matter how irrational they may seem. The district director of one company—we'll call him Smith—felt that status symbols such as office size, furniture, location, etc., were not important. He made sure his people were paid well and he treated them with respect—so why should they be concerned with these details?

But most people *do* care about such things. Consequently, when Smith moved one of his managers from a large corner office to a much more modest one, the manager was upset for weeks.

Smith had no ill intentions. He thought he was taking a rational approach. Office size and placement meant nothing to him, so he couldn't see their importance to anyone else. But if he had used a truly rational approach—that is, one that takes all factors into account, even the illogical ones, so long as they are factors that influence people—he would have given people's feelings their due weight. A number of his people were made unhappy by things that, in the long run, would have cost him very little to avoid.

But what was worse than moving his manager to a smaller office was the fact that Smith didn't respect the man's feelings. We may not be able to give people what they want, but we can at least show them that we understand how they feel. We can't do this if we tell them their feelings are irrational and silly.

Whether you consider it valid or not, if a person feels a particular way about something, that's the way

43

he feels. You can tell him he's not being sensible, but that's not likely to change the way he feels. To ignore his feelings, therefore, even if they are not rational, is in itself irrational!

Assumptions. Another drawback to effective communication is to assume the listener knows much more than he does. Many people are guilty of this mistake. They don't want to insult the person by telling him things he may already know, so they leave things unsaid, often causing confusion.

This is prevalent when people give instructions. They themselves have analyzed the situation thoroughly. They know what the problem is, what led up to it, what the alternative solutions are, and how they want to handle it. But when they present their ideas to someone, they just give him the tip of the iceberg.

A manufacturer's rep in business for himself liked to sleep late, go to his office just before noon, and work until seven at night. The new young secretary he hired knew his work habits and his schedule.

One morning when someone asked for her boss, she said he wasn't in. When asked where the boss was, she said he was home sleeping. Of course, the rep was furious when he came in and heard what had happened. But she thought she had simply stated an innocent fact.

You might expect that a person answering an office phone would not divulge this kind of information. But the young worker, just out of school, had no idea it was wrong. No one had told her.

How often do you assume that people have the same background information that you do? Or the same experience and knowledge? Or the same view of what is appropriate to say? Wouldn't it be better to tell them a little *more,* even if they might already know some of it? Furthermore, a review is useful once in a while for reinforcement and clarification. If you're boring people with repeated information, they can speak up and tell you.

Switches. Because your mind works faster than you can talk, you may often be thinking about a new subject while you're still talking about an old one. So in the middle of a conversation you switch to the new

44

subject. You expect the other person to follow you, but switching is more likely to leave him confused. He tries to relate it to the old conversation—and it probably won't fit:

> BARRY   We've got to do something about this accounts receivable.
>
> LEN   You think we should change the collection procedure?
>
> BARRY   I think we should try some phone calls on the really late accounts.
>
> LEN   Past 90 days?
>
> BARRY   No, I think we shouldn't wait that long. Let's start calling them at 60 days.
>
> LEN   So you want me to call every account that's past 60 days?
>
> BARRY   (He is now thinking that paying a personal visit to the accounts in the local area might be a good idea.) Get me a list of all the local accounts that are past 60 days. I want them called on.
>
> LEN   [Thinking Barry is still talking about phoning] Oh, you just mean local accounts?
>
> BARRY   Anybody in a 90-mile radius of here, and with a minimum account of $500.
>
> LEN   O.K.

At the end of this conversation, Len thinks Barry wants him to compile a list and call only those accounts who are 60 or more days past due, are within a 90-mile radius, and have a minimum account of $500. What Barry actually wants him to do is to start calling every account who is 60 days past due, but to give Barry a list of the special local accounts so Barry can decide if they should be called on personally.

Barry never let Len know that his thoughts were taking a turn. This mess would probably be straightened out before long, but it is an example of what can happen when our minds leap to new trains of thought and we neglect to take the listener along on the ride.

Humor. Humor is fine as long as both parties in the conversation know that that's what it is. This means making very clear to the listener that you are not serious, but are trying to be funny. Subtle humor requires some kind of experiential base or mutual understanding.

If you're not careful, people may take your jests or exaggerated sarcasm seriously. An overly sensitive person may be very hurt by your kidding without your ever realizing it.

The opposite can happen, too. If you have a reputation for being a joker, people may not take you seriously when you want them to.

Kidding someone about their mistakes, for example, and then seriously trying to get them to stop making them, will probably not work very well. They won't notice when you've switched from kidding to meaning it. And when you escalate the seriousness by showing your anger, they'll resent it:

> "Why the hell did he act like it was so funny before if he wanted me to stop doing it?"

Solidifying Your Opinions. Before stating an opinion, your mind is probably open to several alternatives. But stating an opinion is like pouring concrete: Once the words are out, your position hardens. (And writing the opinion solidifies it even more.)

Once you've spoken for a particular point of view, there's a tendency to stick with it—even if you yourself weren't entirely sold on it at the beginning. The fact that you've *said* it makes you take a position and defend it. After all, who wants to be told, "But that's not what you said yesterday."

This is too bad, because new facts and input are entering your brain all the time. If you didn't feel you had to defend your old opinions, you could allow yourself the flexibility of forming better ones. Rather than being a sign of weakness, the ability to change one's stated opinions is a sensible, mature way of dealing with our ever-changing world.

Maintaining Communication Lines. Communication isn't something you can leave packed away until you need it. If you have largely ignored a subordinate for the six months he's been with you, don't expect to have him receive you as an old buddy on the day you decide to have a heart-to-heart talk with him. It takes time and effort to establish open communication lines, to build trust, to get to know each other.

There was a time when it was fashionable to put down small talk as meaningless, a waste of time. And in the name of efficiency you may wonder what good it does to ask a worker how he or she is feeling or how his kids are doing at school. But as psychologists have pointed out (and as most people have known all along), small talk makes us feel comfortable with one another. It's an acknowledgment of the other's existence and importance—and of the fact that we all face pretty much the same human struggle. The boss who only talks business soon gets a reputation for being a machine, not a person.

A public accountant recently pointed this out to a partner of her firm. A lot of the young, bright accountants were leaving the firm instead of sticking with it and trying to make partner themselves some day. This woman suggested to the partner that the only image his employees had of him and the other partners was that they did nothing but work all the time. She suggested he talk more about his home and his family, letting the younger people see that he indeed had a life outside the company. She was quite pleased a few days later to overhear this partner discussing his dog and his house with one of the young accountants.

Steps to More Effective Talking

1. Make sure you have your listener's attention before you begin your message.
2. Point out any possible benefits of your message— give the listener a reason for *wanting* to hear you.
3. Suit your language to your listener. Don't use terms that are too technical, sentences that are too complex, or ideas that are too abstract. On the other hand, don't oversimplify or talk down to people—they'll resent it.
4. Be aware of emotional blocks to listening. For

example, if people are under stress or suspect your motives, they won't hear you clearly.

5. Try to start from a base of mutual understanding and agreement. Keep tuned in to your listener's point of view.

6. Don't expect to win people over with reason and logic. You might win an argument, but you won't change a person's *feelings* that way.

7. Don't lean on policy and rules. Give people reasons *why* a rule is a rule. Don't be afraid to bend the rules when it makes sense.

8. Respect people's feelings, no matter how irrational they seem.

9. Don't assume people have the same frame of reference and background you do. Fill them in. Tell them *more* than they need to know, if necessary, but not *less*.

10. Watch out when your mind switches to a new subject. Be sure to let your listener know you're on a new track.

11. Be careful that people don't misread your humor. If you like to kid people sarcastically, watch out that you're not actually hurting someone who's especially sensitive and takes it the wrong way.

12. Don't use humor when it's not appropriate. People may not like it if you first kid them about undesirable behavior and then seriously criticize them for it.

13. Avoid the tendency to become wedded to an opinion merely because you've said it or written it. Don't be afraid to say, "I changed my mind."

14. Keep communication lines open. Be willing for the people under you to know that you laugh and cry and bleed just like they do.

Straight Talking

In an article on managerial communication, Herb Genfan says that messages are requests: "When a manager, at any level, and in any organization, talks or writes to an employee, colleague, boss or client, he is asking the message receiver to do or believe something he, the manager, wants. He is asking the receiver

48

to say, in effect, 'Yes, I'll do that,' or, 'Yes, I'll act on your information from now on.' " *

Another way to look at communication is to think of the possible effect it can have—the change it makes in the receiver. A message could change the way you feel about things, the way you think about things (your opinions), the way you see things, or the way you do things (resulting in some action).

If there is no change in the receiver, or a change other than the intended one, the communication hasn't worked. Something interfered between the intent and the result. Maybe the listener wasn't paying attention. Maybe there were conflicting signals, misunderstanding of terms, prejudice, prior opinions—any of the things we've talked about in the previous pages.

How often have you heard, "But I thought you said . . .," or, "That's not what I meant . . ."? If you were dealing with a machine, you could punch a particular key and know that the machine recorded your message accurately. But people—they have years of preconceptions, feelings, ideas of their own. There is no way to force-feed information into the brain of a person.

In addition to all the problems of listening and talking discussed so far is the avoidance of responsibility for the message. This underlies many management communication difficulties. And it leads to talking in circles:

> At four o'clock in the afternoon, Kelly's boss dumped a rush project in her lap. There was no way Kelly could get it out in time unless she had Sharon work overtime on it. But at coffee break that morning Sharon had told Kelly she was having company for supper that night. So how could Kelly rightfully ask Sharon to work overtime?

Here is what resulted:

> KELLY   Boy, Jack just dumped this Anderson project on me. I've got to give it to

* Genfan, Herb. "Managerial Communication." *Personnel Journal,* November 1976.

	him at eight o'clock tomorrow morning. [Please volunteer to help me out, Sharon.]
SHARON	That's tough. [God, I hope she doesn't ask me to stay overtime.]
KELLY	Yeah, and all the rest of the staff are already working overtime on other rush stuff. [C'mon, Sharon—help me out.]
SHARON	Why don't you tell Jack there's just no way to do it? [And get off my back!]
KELLY	[Don't tell me what to tell Jack! Who's supervisor here, anyway!?] Listen, Sharon, Jack told me to get it out because it's important—and there's only one way to get it done.
SHARON	[Oh, the high-and-mighty routine—and she tries to make me think she's my friend!] And what's that? [said in a sarcastic tone]
KELLY	[If that's her attitude, she needs to be put in her place!] You'll work overtime to get it done! [said in an angry tone of voice]

What happened here? Kelly wanted Sharon to work overtime to finish the Anderson project, but Kelly didn't want to have to *ask* Sharon to do this because she knew Sharon wouldn't want to do it. Sharon might not *like* Kelly if she asks her to work overtime.

So Kelly talks in circles. She hints at the problem, hoping Sharon will volunteer to work overtime and take her off the hook.

But what were the results? Worse than if Kelly had said straight out:

"Sharon, I hate to ask you this, but I want you to work overtime tonight on a rush project that just came in."

Sharon won't like it, but at least she won't feel manipulated by Kelly as she does in the first dialogue.

50

And she'll know that Kelly feels bad about asking her. Look again at the straight-talking statement Kelly might have made; you'll see that it has three primary parts:

I (Kelly, the sender)
want you (Sharon, the receiver)
to work overtime (the request)

This is a simple model, and should be easy to follow when making requests. But as Genfan points out, "Many managers deny *they* are sending the message, deny they are *requesting* something, or even deny they requested something of *someone*."

Why would a manager avoid straight talking? Because she might hurt someone's feelings. Because people might not like her. Because they might say "no."

The trouble is, talking in circles doesn't help avoid conflicts. It only gets the manager into more trouble. She gets the reputation of being a person who beats around the bush, or tries to manipulate people. They say, "You never know where you stand with her."

She expects people to read her mind and know what she wants. But people can't really read her mind. And it makes them nervous trying. One day when Kelly casually tells Sharon that a big job has been dumped on her, and no intention of asking anything of Sharon, the latter—anxious, nervous, unable to guess what Kelly wants—will start to get hostile and defensive, misinterpreting Kelly's intent.

It's a not-so-merry-go-round, because Kelly's circular talking makes Sharon careful about what she says in Kelly's presence. It's better to be a bull who tells people what he wants them to do in no uncertain terms than to talk in circles. People can learn to deal with a consistent manager through trial and error. But a manager who engages in circular talking—who talks sweet one minute, hides his intentions the next, and gets angry when people don't read his mind properly —increases the levels of hostility and anxiety all around him.

If you don't like giving people assignments they resent, you can express your feelings and still talk straight: "Sharon, I hate to ask you this . . ." "Bill, I understand how you feel about working overtime . . ." "John, I'm not happy about this either . . ."

But express these feelings only when they are valid. Don't imagine that by prefacing every unpleasant assignment with regret you can make up for its unpleasantness. And even when you legitimately feel bad about giving out a miserable assignment, your subordinates may not be too sympathetic to your feelings. After all, *they* are getting the rotten assignment. The best situation would be if they could express *their* feelings, perhaps like this: "Frankly, I don't enjoy getting this assignment, but if it has to be done, I'll do it."

Whatever way your subordinate expresses his or her dissatisfaction, don't let it upset you. The more he can get off his chest at the time, the less likely it is that bad feelings will linger.

And don't go overboard in expressing your bad feelings. You may be tempted to do this to ease your own conscience, but it's not an effective way of managing. It's important for you to be firm, to give the employee the idea right away that you have made up your mind and that the assignment *must* be carried out. If you get too gushy about how you hate to ask him to do the job, you're inviting him to think he might be able to get out of it.

A small manufacturer of hand-crafted goods was disturbed by the mess in which his employees left the work-room: tools out, unfinished work on the benches, scraps on the floor, etc. At first he said nothing and just hoped they would change their ways. But they didn't.

Finally, one afternoon at quitting time, as people were leaving, he walked through the work area and said, "What a mess this place is in!" He picked up a broom and started sweeping, to set a good example. A couple of people looked sheepish as they waved goodbye, but no one pitched in.

Finally, exasperated, he walked into the work area one quitting time and said, "I'm sick and tired of cleaning up after you people! I want this place spotless before anyone leaves!" They stayed and cleaned up, but they weren't very happy about having to work past quitting time. The next day, and for a few days after that, they quit early to clean up. But gradually, as no more mention was made of the subject, they went back to their old habits.

Never once did this manager say calmly, simply, and directly what he wanted.

Some managers are so afraid of talking straight to their employees that they would rather have to fire someone than deal with the day-to-day responsibility of getting them to do their jobs right. They'll hint and complain and hope that the person catches on and shapes up. When the subordinate still doesn't improve, they say: "I tried. I gave him plenty of opportunity to get his act together." But this is merely shirking a manager's responsibility.

Another way to avoid responsibility is to put the blame someplace else:

"*They* want it done this way."
"The *customer* will cancel if you don't get out there today."
"*Accounting* wants you to fill out this form."

A manager may talk circularly when speaking to his boss and co-workers, too. It's just as ineffective there:

RALPH	It sure is hard to balance the budget these days. [I can't on the money you pay me]
RALPH'S BOSS	You're not kidding. My wife has given up trying. [You're not the only one suffering, Ralph]
RALPH	With inflation, a person can't keep up with the cost of living. [Especially with the measly raise you gave me]
RALPH'S BOSS	I know exactly what you mean. [You're not going to make me feel guilty]
RALPH	And with the taxes they take out, a thousand-dollar raise doesn't go very far. [I deserved at least *two* thousand]

RALPH'S BOSS	That's true, it's getting worse all the time. [I can keep this up as long as you can]
RALPH	I don't know how I'm going to manage this year. [You heartless bum!]
RALPH'S BOSS	It's tough on everyone these days. [Stands up, informing Ralph that the conversation is over]

Maybe Ralph wouldn't have gotten a bigger raise if he'd come out and asked for it, but feelings on both sides would have been better. This conversation left both of them with a bad taste.

Take Responsibility for Your Message:

1. Talk straight, putting the "I" where it belongs:
   "I want"
   "I need"
   "I don't like"
2. Tell people exactly what you want. Don't beat around the bush:
   "I want more money," not, "It's tough living on my salary"
3. If you want someone to do something, tell that person:
   "I want you to deliver this package," not
   "Someone's got to get this package delivered."
4. Don't expect people to read your mind, take your hints, or share your values.
5. If you feel bad about giving an unpleasant assignment, it's O.K. to express this feeling briefly:
   "I'm sorry to spoil your evening, Fred, but I need you to work overtime tonight."

Nonverbal Messages

Just as important as the actual words you use are the nonverbal messages you send. These messages are transmitted through eye contact, body posture, gestures, facial expressions, tone of voice, and timing.

Look at these three ways of saying to the boss, "I'd like to talk to you about a raise."

1. You walk up to the boss's office, but stand hesitatingly in the doorway until he calls you in. You stand far back from his desk, talk in a low voice, and look at the floor while you talk. One hand fondles the buttons on your jacket, while you stand sideways and slightly stooped over.

2. You barge into the boss's office without knocking or waiting for him to ask you in. You lean menacingly over him, pound your fist on the table, and speak in a loud tone of voice. You glare at him and set your jaw firmly.

3. You knock on the boss's door. When he asks you in, you walk briskly up to his desk, look him steadily in the eye, and speak in a conversational tone of medium volume. You smiled pleasantly when you came in, then faced him squarely to talk.

Which nonverbal message would you expect to be the most effective?

Assertive eye contact doesn't mean aggressive staring. A relaxed, steady gaze, with occasional looking away, is the most natural and comfortable.

Robert E. Alberti and Michael L. Emmons point out in their book *Stand Up, Speak Out, Talk Back!* * that a message accented with the appropriate gestures takes on added emphasis. Using your hands and arms in a natural way to emphasize particular points shows that you're relaxed and in control of the situation. Folding the arms or hanging them stiffly at your side, or nervous gesturing, like playing with a piece of jewelry or clothing, have the opposite effect. If you can develop expressive gestures that match your words, they'll help punctuate the verbal message.

Your facial expressions should also match your message. Compliant people often are afraid to express anger, so they smile when they're angry with someone. This contradicts the message they're trying to get across and gives away their nervousness.

What Kind of Nonverbal Messages Do You Give? To get a better feel for facial expressions, stand in front of a mirror and make faces. Watch what hap-

* Alberti, Robert E., and Emmons, Michael L. *Stand Up, Speak Out, Talk Back!* Pocket Books, 1970.

pens to your facial muscles when you pretend to feel joy, anger, etc. How does it feel when you express these feelings?

Voice, tone, and pitch are also important. The person who mumbles is probably afraid to say what's on his mind. Not saying it loud enough is almost like not saying it at all. It doesn't work, and this person only frustrates those around him who can't hear and have to keep saying "What?" all the time.

Nonassertive people are likely to end statements by trailing off into nothingness, or, if making a request, ending on an upbeat instead of a downbeat. How would you make this statement: "I'd like to take a vacation day Thursday." Clearly and firmly all the way through? Or would you phrase it as a question?

Use a tape recorder to check your own voice pitch and loudness. Make each of the following statements in various ways: loud and angry sounding; soft and questioning; moderate and conversationally:

1. I'M VERY HAPPY TO MEET YOU.
2. I DON'T LIKE THAT.
3. I'M REALLY ANGRY WITH YOU.
4. I WANT A RAISE.
5. I'M SORRY.
6. I WANT YOU TO DO THAT OVER AGAIN.
7. WOULD YOU PUT OUT YOUR CIGARETTE?
   IT IRRITATES ME.
8. YOU DID A GREAT JOB.
9. WE DON'T HAVE IT IN STOCK.

How did your voice tone and volume change in each of the messages? Were you able to *really* sound angry when you said Number 3? Where you able to say Number 5 as though you meant it?

To help control your body language, gestures, facial expression, and voice, visualize the way you want to appear. Suppose you are planning a talk with the boss about a raise, a new project, a problem. Imagine how you would like to walk, talk, and feel while you're having the discussion. Then picture yourself doing it that way.

If you're planning a speech or presentation in which

you wish to appear confident and assertive, practice first in front of a mirror, and with a tape recorder. Then, if possible, give the talk in front of friends or family and ask them for their impressions. Use the following questions to help them analyze your speech:

1. Did I talk too fast or too slowly?
2. Was my voice too loud or too soft?
3. Did I appear calm and collected, or nervous?
4. Was I too stiff?
5. Did I use appropriate gestures, or were they distracting?
6. How was my posture? Did I stand erect, but naturally, or did I slump?
7. Did I make eye contact with you, or stare above your head or down at the floor?
8. Did I speak in a monotone or in a sing-song way? Did I use my voice to emphasize important points?
9. Did I pause appropriately for emphasis, or rush from one point to the next?
10. Overall, did I come across as someone who is self-confident and knowledgeable in my subject area?

You may want to provide this checklist at the beginning of your presentation so that your listeners can take notes. Then use their feedback to work on the trouble spots. Practice may not make perfect, but it can help a lot.

The Clothes You Wear. While it isn't necessary to wear any particular type of clothes to act assertive, you may find that you personally are affected by it. Basically, it's a matter of how you feel about yourself. If you *feel* that you're not as well-dressed as your peers in the office, you may *act* as if you are less worthy than they.

This is one reason people who want to achieve executive positions are advised to dress like executives. In addition to making other people think better of them, it makes them feel better about themselves.

Try an experiment. One day wear the best suit or outfit you've got, the one that makes you look good as well as businesslike. Observe how you carry yourself and interact with people that day. The next day, wear something from the other end of the line—something that's barely passable, doesn't flatter you, and, if anything, makes you look fit for a lower position in the company. How do you act and feel dressed like this?

Perhaps some people can walk into an office dressed in dungarees and feel like an executive, but most of us can't. (At least, not unless we own the company.)

Persistence Pays Off

This technique sounds simple, and it is. It's also amazingly effective. Yet people don't use it much. So if you *do*, you'll be way ahead of the game.

Consider the child who wants a cookie:

CHILD   Can I have a cookie?
PARENT   No.
CHILD   Can't I *please*?
PARENT   I said no, and I meant it.
CHILD   But I'm hungry. I want a cookie.
PARENT   You'll spoil your appetite for supper.
CHILD   Just *one* cookie?
PARENT   Oh, all right—but just *one.*

Children know the value of persistence. They know that eventually they'll wear their parents down.

Well, the same technique can be used in any conflict situation. You want something. You ask for it. The other person says "no." You ask again. And again. And again. Eventually it will mean more to him to get rid of you than to keep you from getting what you want.

Here are some examples of how persistence pays off on the job:

Joe needs to hire a new worker immediately. He calls Charlie in Personnel to ask him to get someone as soon as possible.

JOE   Hi, Charlie. I've got an emergency situation here and need a worker right

58

	away. Do you have anyone to send me?
CHARLIE	There's no one available now, Joe. I'll see what I can do.
JOE	Charlie, I need someone *now*.
CHARLIE	Listen, there are ten people ahead of you. I can only do so much.
JOE	When will you have someone for me? I need them right away.
CHARLIE	I'll do what I can, but I can't promise anything.
JOE	Will you have someone for me by Friday? That's as long as I can wait. We're really short and I need someone badly.
CHARLIE	I'll try to have someone for you by Friday.
JOE	O.K. I'll be counting on you.

This conversation occurs on Monday. On Tuesday, Joe calls Charlie again:

JOE	Hi, Charlie. How are you doing on getting some help for me?
CHARLIE	Gee, Joe, it's only Tuesday. I haven't had a chance to do anything yet.
JOE	I really need a guy badly. Will you have someone for me by Friday?
CHARLIE	I'll do my best.

By now, Charlie is anxious to do anything necessary to get Joe off his back. If not, another phone call on Wednesday should do the trick.

The important thing in this technique is to remain calm and repeat your wants in a conversational, pleasant tone, but not to allow yourself to be sidetracked. Stick to your point, no matter what the other person says.

A co-worker, Stella, is always asking Harriet to donate to some charity or other. Harriet always has given something in the past, but this time she decides she does not want to contribute.

STELLA	Hi, Harriet. I'm collecting for the People for Porpoises Society. How much can I put you down for?
HARRIET	Nothing, Stella. I don't want to contribute.
STELLA	What? Did I catch you short? I'll come back on payday.
HARRIET	No, I'm not short. I just don't want to contribute.
STELLA	But do you realize what will happen to porpoises all over the world if we don't help them? Right now while we're talking, *thousands* of them are being destroyed! Mercilessly! Can you picture that?
HARRIET	I understand how you feel, Stella, but I still don't want to contribute.
STELLA	How will you sleep at night if you don't do something to help them?
HARRIET	I just don't want to contribute, Stella.
STELLA	Are you mad at me or something, Harriet?
HARRIET	No, Stella. I don't want to contribute to this cause.
STELLA	But I don't understand . . . you always give when I come around collecting.
HARRIET	That's true, I have in the past, but I don't want to contribute to this cause. Try me again sometime. I may or may not want to contribute to the next one.

Even though Harriet had always felt suckered into Stella's causes in the past, and *obliged* to contribute something, she didn't allow herself to be bulldozed again. By repeating the simple message, "I don't want to," in a calm tone of voice, she eventually came through. Feeling confident by the end of the conversation, she even invited Stella to try her again in the future. This allows Harriet to give to the causes she wishes to, and to refuse if she feels like it. This will

60

also give her additional practice in being assertive. And Stella won't go off thinking Harriet is angry with her.

Carol wants her new secretary, Lena, to make wider margins on the letters she types.

> CAROL   Lena, would you redo these letters with wider margins, please? I like all my letters to have at least a one-inch margin on all sides.
> LENA   O.K.

Lena does the letters over, with wider margins, but the next day again brings in a batch of letters with narrow margins.

> CAROL   Lena, I like my letters to have margins of at least one inch. Here, if you'll look at this ruler, you'll see that these margins are only a half inch to three quarters of an inch wide. Would you retype them, please, with one-inch margins?
> LENA   All right.

The next day Lena brings in another batch of letters. Most of them have at least one-inch margins, but two very long letters have half-inch margins.

> CAROL   Lena, most of these letters have the margins just the way I asked for them —at least one inch. But these two have narrower margins. I like *all* my letters to have margins of at least one inch. Would you do them over, please?
> LENA   But they'll be too long if I make such wide margins.
> CAROL   I'm sure they will be longer if you make wider margins, but I like all margins to be at least one inch. From now on would you measure all the margins and make sure they're at least

	one inch before you give the letters
	to me?
LENA	Can't these go out the way they are
	and next time I'll make them wider?
CAROL	No, I like all my letters to go out with
	margins of at least one inch. Would
	you please do them over?
LENA	O.K.
CAROL	Thank you.

This may seem to be a picky issue, but very often these are the kinds of things that can drive you nuts. Carol could have shut up about the margins, thinking it was a small issue and Lena was having a rough enough time breaking into her new job. But since it did bother Carol, she would continue to be irritated and might have eventually exploded.

No matter how small something seems, if it's important to you, it's important to you. You don't have to justify its importance. From your persistently asking for what you want, and not settling for less, the other person will eventually figure out that it's easier to give you what you want than to continue resisting.

Mary, a first-level supervisor, wants to go to a seminar on management training in order to prepare herself to move up. She approaches her boss.

MARY	Hi, Harry. Do you have a minute?
HARRY	Sure, Mary. What's up?
MARY	I've been a supervisor for six months
	now, Harry, and I really enjoy man-
	aging people.
HARRY	I'm glad you're happy. You've been
	doing a great job.
MARY	Thanks. I hope to continue moving
	up in management here; that's what I
	want to talk to you about. I need
	more training in management skills,
	and there's a great seminar next
	month at City College I'd like to
	attend.
HARRY	Oh? You mean during work hours?

62

MARY   Yes. It's a three-day seminar and costs $100. I'd like to go to it.

HARRY   But who's going to do your job while you're out?

MARY   Phyllis could handle things while I'm gone. I'll see that things are in good shape before I leave. I really want to go to that seminar.

HARRY   Our education budget is all used up for this quarter, Mary. I'm sorry.

MARY   Can I go to one next quarter then?

HARRY   We'll see.

After Mary leaves Harry she tries to find out what seminars will be available the following quarter. The next week she brings in a brochure about another seminar.

MARY   There's a seminar coming up the following quarter that sounds great. I'd like to go to it.

HARRY   Well, I can't promise you anything. Lots of people want to go to seminars and conferences, and we only have so much money.

MARY   When will I be able to go to a seminar?

HARRY   I'll let you know.

But Mary persists. Every couple of weeks she tells Harry about a seminar she's heard about and how much she wants to get some management training. After a while, he says she can go just to get rid of her.

One of our students told us this story about how persistence paid off:

"I was promoted to a rank where normally you would get your own office. However, they just left me sitting out at the desk where I had been before. And there wasn't enough room for the new files I needed. That was the main thing that bothered me—plus the prestige factor.

"So I went to the man in charge of room assignments and told him I wanted an office. He said that even though I had been promoted, I would have to stay where I was for another year.

"I explained to him that I didn't have sufficient space for my files, and I mentioned that a couple of partners required me to keep their clients' files nearby so I could service them quickly. After this explanation, he said he would look into getting me another file.

"I let a week go by and nothing happened. Then I went back to him and said that if I couldn't have a file, I wanted a credenza. I also pointed out that there were empty offices around and that I would personally make the arrangements to get my things moved. But he said 'No' again.

"So I just kept at him. I called him every week. Finally he realized it was easier to give me the room."

Here is how to cope with another kind of situation:

A new procedure has been instituted for operating the gidget machine. Sam had a meeting with all his people to discuss the new method, at which time everyone's questions and doubts were answered. At this meeting, Bernie said he didn't think the new method was better, even after Sam explained it as best he could. Bernie said he didn't like it and refused to accept Sam's reasoning. Sam ended this part of the discussion by saying that even though Bernie disagreed, he still had to use the new procedure, like everyone else. Now they have started using the new method. All except Bernie, who continues to do it the old way.

When Sam comes by Bernie's work station, he sees Bernie using the old procedure.

SAM   Bernie, I see you're still using the old procedure on the gidget machine. I want you to start using the new procedure.

BERNIE   I don't like it.

SAM   I understand how you feel, Bernie, but I still want you to start using the new procedure.

BERNIE   I've been working here 30 years and we always did it this way.

SAM   That's true Bernie, but now you've got
        to change and do it the new way.
BERNIE O.K., O.K. [He starts doing it the new
        way, and Sam leaves.]

Sam comes back later that day and sees Bernie doing
things the old way again.

SAM   Bernie, I want you to use the new
        procedure even when I'm not watch-
        ing you.
BERNIE I'm sorry, I forgot. I just can't get
        used to it. After 30 years you auto-
        matically revert to what you've been
        doing all your life.
SAM   I understand that, Bernie, but I want
        you to start using the new procedure
        and to keep using it.
BERNIE I'll try. [He switches to new proce-
        dure. Sam watches him for a few
        minutes, then leaves.]

An hour later Sam returns to Bernie's work area and
sees that he's using the new method.

SAM   I'm glad to see you using the new
        procedure, Bernie. That's what I want.
BERNIE Right.

The next day when Sam stops by Bernie's work area,
Bernie is again back to the old procedure.

SAM   Bernie, I want you to keep using the
        new procedure—every day—all day.
BERNIE Oh, when I came in this morning I
        forgot all about it. [He continues to
        use old procedure.]
SAM   Would you start using the new pro-
        cedure, Bernie? I want you to keep
        at it.
BERNIE O.K., if that's what you want. [He
        switches to the new procedure.] But
        it takes me longer to make the gidgets

	this way, you know. My production's going to be way off with this.
SAM	I understand your problem, but I want you to use the new method anyway.
BERNIE	Don't you care about production?
SAM	I want you to use the new procedure, Bernie.
BERNIE	When your father was supervisor here, he wouldn't pull something like this.
SAM	That may be true, but I still want you to use the new procedure, Bernie.
BERNIE	Well, I don't like it!
SAM	You don't have to like it, Bernie, but I want you to do it.
BERNIE	Don't you have anything else to do all day but stand here and tell me to use the new procedure?
SAM	Lots of things, but I still want you to use the new procedure.
BERNIE	[laughs] All right, you win.

Note how Bernie tried to manipulate Sam: threatening him with lowered production and comparing him to his father. But Sam didn't argue with Bernie or allow himself to get sidetracked. He just kept pushing his point. When Bernie finally realized he was beaten, he laughed at the situation to relieve the tension.

Also note that at one point when Bernie *was* using the new procedure, Sam reinforced this behavior by telling him he was glad to see him using it. With someone a little less stubborn than Bernie, this might have been all that was necessary.

If Bernie continued to be a problem . . . if Sam came back a week or month later and found him reverting to the old method . . . Sam could continue the persistent approach until Bernie gave up.

What happens if Bernie is more persistent than Sam? This is unlikely, since Bernie knows he's in the weaker position. At any point he could be fired for not following orders. But he's a good worker, so naturally Sam doesn't want to get anywhere near this point. If he allowed Bernie to have his way, however, Sam's authority would be weakened—with Bernie and with the other workers who see Bernie getting away with it.

Assertive persistence is probably the handiest supervisory tool there is, yet most managers don't use it as much as they should. They let themselves be worn down by stubborn subordinates like Bernie. Or they become angry and threatening.

Other managers think that they've got to get subordinates to *accept the manager's point of view*. This is fine when it can be done. But discussions about the validity of the new procedure would have been wasted on Bernie. He just didn't want to change. But as Sam told him, "You don't have to like it, you just have to do it."

How to Persist

1. Phrase your request in a direct statement: I want you to . . .
2. Speak in a calm, conversational, but firm voice. No matter what the other person says, don't become excited or angry.
3. Keep repeating the message.
4. Don't let yourself be sidetracked by other issues, excuses, accusations, etc.
5. Get a commitment. If the person says "maybe," or "soon," try to pin him down to a specific date when you'll get what you want.
6. Follow up to make sure the person is doing what you asked him or her to. Come back as many times as necessary until it is done.

Workable Compromise

Perhaps you noticed that the end result in some of the "Persistence" examples was a compromise. Mary wasn't able to go to the first seminar she wanted to attend, but eventually she got to one. If she merely had stood her ground on the first request, repeating over and over again that she wanted to go to *that particular* seminar, no matter what, chances are Harry would have kicked her out of his office and maybe even out of her job.

Joe wanted Charlie to find a worker for him at once —but was willing to compromise by giving Charlie until the end of the week.

But Carol wasn't willing to compromise by allowing Lena to send out even one letter without the one-inch margins. There was no intrinsic right and wrong here. Carol could just as well have said, "O.K., you can send these letters out, but from now on I want them to have one-inch margins." By not compromising in this situation, however, Lena will be more likely to make the margins one inch in the future.

Sam couldn't very well compromise with Bernie. It was either the new procedure or the old one. Only by insisting that Bernie change at once would Sam ever get him to change.

Whether you are able to work out a compromise, and what kind of compromise you work out, will depend on the situation. Manuel Smith points out in *When I Say No, I Feel Guilty* * that it is practical, whenever your self-respect isn't in question, to offer a workable compromise.

Some people find it difficult to handle the compromise. For a nonassertive person, it's much easier to stand firm on a single line than to manage the negotiation of a compromise. A friend of ours always says "No" to everything in order to avoid the responsibility of figuring out which things he'd really like to say "Yes" to.

Another way to handle this is always to respond "I'll think about it" when anyone asks you to do something. That gives you time to get in touch with your feelings and decide what you want to do.

But on the job there are many situations in which you have to make decisions and work out compromises on the spot. If you're relaxed and can evaluate the situation easily, there's no problem: Go with the way you feel.

But how many times have you walked out of the boss's office, or left a conversation with a co-worker, thinking, "Why did I say that?"

* Smith, Manuel J. *When I Say No, I Feel Guilty*. Bantam Books, 1975.

You might have walked in with a great plan, well rehearsed and airtight. But after the third sentence the other person threw in an objection you hadn't prepared for. Suddenly you're in deep water. You automatically react to the remark, giving in or saying something you wouldn't have if you'd had a chance to think about it.

Let's look at Harriet and Stella again, rewriting the scene. Harriet sees Stella coming with her collection plate and stops her before she can say anything:

HARRIET   Stella, you can skip me today. I'm not contributing anything.

STELLA   Oh, but wait 'til you hear what it's for.

HARRIET   [interrupting] I don't care what it's for—I'm sick and tired of your collections and that's that.

STELLA   But it's to buy a present for the boss in the hospital.

HARRIET   I said I don't care what it's for.

STELLA   All right, all right.

Harriet worked herself up to the point where she could not hear anything Stella said. Harriet programmed herself to say "No" and couldn't allow any compromise. If she really didn't care, and didn't want to contribute to the boss's present . . . fine. But suppose she really would have liked to contribute?

Let's look at Joe and Charlie again. Suppose it happened this way:

JOE   Charlie, I need a worker badly. Do you have anyone you can send me?

CHARLIE   Nope.

JOE   Well, when can you get me someone? I need them right away.

CHARLIE   There's nothing I can do for you until next month. Get some temporary help in.

JOE   What do you mean?

CHARLIE   Call Manpower or one of those other temporary agencies. I'll have my secretary give you the numbers. Hold on.

69

And Charlie puts Joe on "hold." After he has taken the telephone numbers from Charlie's secretary, Joe sits there thinking to himself: "What am I doing? I don't want to hire a temporary worker for this job—it takes too much training. What I need is a permanent person, and soon. Why the hell did I agree to this?"

It looks as though Harriet and Joe are in a bind. They both said things they didn't mean because they were taken by surprise. What can they do now?

Actually, it's very simple. Harriet goes up to Stella and says: "Here's $5.00 toward the boss's gift, Stella. *I changed my mind.*"

Joe calls Charlie back and says: "Charlie, thanks for the temporary agency's phone numbers, but I need a permanent employee." Then Joe can continue the persistent verbal technique he had planned to use in the first place. He keeps bugging Charlie until he gets results. If no results are possible—e.g., the president of the company decreed there will be no hiring for a month—then there's nothing Joe can do. He's done his best.

At this point in assertiveness training some people usually are saying to themselves:

"But what will people think if I change my mind, agreeing with something one minute and then coming back and saying something different?"

Does it matter what they think? Is that more important than getting what you want? Remember your rights as a human being: the right to be wrong, the right to be illogical.

Here's another way to look at it: Changing your mind doesn't mean that your revised opinion is wrong. Wouldn't Joe have given a worse impression if he had gone ahead and hired a temporary worker for this job? Wouldn't Harriet have suffered more by being the only person in the office not to contribute to the boss's present?

Whenever you say something you really can't accept, give an opinion you don't hold, or agree to do something you can't do—it's better to look a little silly

70

changing your mind than to follow through with the original bad move.

If you're not naturally assertive, and have difficulty thinking on your feet, so to speak, changing your mind is a way to get around your difficulty. As you practice and assertiveness becomes more natural to you, you won't have to do it as often. But in the beginning it's reassuring to know you don't have to be perfect, even in being assertive. You can goof up and say the wrong thing, make the wrong decision, and go back and correct it.

In working out compromises, be careful you don't give in too quickly. Keep repeating your original request in spite of what the other person says. This gives the impression you can't be manipulated, and it gets past the person's initial excuses. Now he or she probably will be ready to make a more realistic counter-offer. At this point, you may want to accept it.

Also take into consideration whom you're dealing with. If you're talking to someone who always gives you a straight answer about what he can or cannot do, it makes sense to work out a compromise early. But if you're dealing with someone whose style is to manipulate every chance he gets, you'll have to be more firm, compromising only after you're certain all the tricks are out of the bag.

How can you tell the difference between people? The manipulator often has a different excuse each time you persist. He's likely to try to make you feel guilty, or foolish, or stupid. He may appeal to rules, or a higher authority, or some vague "right way" that things must be done.

The open, straight talker, on the other hand, usually will give you the real reason he can or cannot do something right off. He will stick to this reason whether it works or not, rather than manufacture new reasons.

Can you tell which is which in the following dialogues?

> JACK   I want this report out by the first of the month.
>
> SUSAN   You're kidding! You know it will take me longer than that!

JACK	I hope not, Susan, because I want it the first of the month.
SUSAN	This kind of report always takes six weeks.
JACK	Whatever it usually takes, this time I want it by the first of the month.
SUSAN	But it'll take me three weeks just to get the computer output on it.
JACK	I'll work with you on that problem, but I want the report the first of the month.
SUSAN	You'd better check with Weber. He'll tell you that we just don't do these reports that fast. It's ridiculous.
JACK	When you're ready to work out the details, let me know, but I expect the finished report on my desk on October first.
SUSAN	You're serious, aren't you?
JACK	Yup.

JACK	I want this report out by the first of the month.
JILL	Gosh, that's going to be rough!
JACK	It may be, but I want it the first of the month.
JILL	I'll do my best, Jack, but I've never been able to get the data I need from the computer group in less than three weeks. That won't give me much time to sum up the results.
JACK	I'll work with you on the computer problem.
JILL	O.K. Can we start on it right now? Here's the problem . . .

Who was more manipulative, Jill or Susan?

Susan may have been right about the computer problem—but how was Jack to know when she brought up so many other issues with it? Look how long it took before Susan realized she was going to have to deal directly with Jack and face the issue squarely.

Jill, on the other hand, went directly to the main

72

issue—the computer problem—and stated it without making it sound as though she was uncooperative. Once Jack discussed this problem with her, he might then decide to extend the report deadline or find some way to get the computer printout faster, or eliminate some of the computer research, if necessary. But at least his choice would be based on the real problem and possible solutions. He'd know that Jill wasn't simply resisting him.

How much assertive persistence you need will depend a lot on the people with whom you're dealing. Some will respond to your first request and do their best to cooperate with you. You won't have to bug such people continually.

Through experience, you'll discover which people need more pushing than others. But sometimes even the open, helpful people will have so many demands made on their time that they tend to grease the squeaky wheel first.

When you're feeling relaxed enough to know and say what you want, and you're pretty sure you're past the baloney, working out a compromise is possible. Here are some situations in which two people decide to compromise constructively on a point of conflict:

Tim is being interviewed for a job opening. Vic has decided to hire him and is at the point of making him an offer.

> VIC Tim, we'd like to have you join our company. I can offer you $10,000 to start.
> TIM I'm really glad to get your offer and want very much to work with Gladco, but $14,000 is what I want to make.
> VIC I'm afraid we can't go that high, Tim.
> TIM What's the best you could offer?
> VIC $12,000 would be tops.
> TIM And when would I be reviewed for a raise?
> VIC In six months.
> TIM O.K., I can accept that.
> VIC Good.

73

Jim wants Bill to work overtime tomorrow night.

JIM	Bill, I'd like you to put in two hours of overtime tomorrow night.
BILL	Gee, I've got a date tomorrow night. Isn't there someone else who could do it?
JIM	The whole shift is working overtime. But we need you, too.
BILL	I could manage one hour, but not two.
JIM	I really need you two hours.
BILL	Hey, how about if I come in an hour early tomorrow and stay one hour at night?
JIM	That'll be fine.

Carol wants to run a $100,000 direct-mail campaign for a product usually not sold in this manner. She has presented a report on her idea to her boss, and they are now at the confrontation stage.

AL	Carol, I'm afraid your idea is too risky. We've never sold Blipos through direct mail, and we'd be taking too big a chance.
CAROL	But the research I've done on similar products shows that Blipos lend themselves very well to direct mail.
AL	I know . . . you've done a good job in your report. But we just can't go for $100,000.
CAROL	Al, I'm so sure this will work, I'd stake my job on it.
AL	I understand how you feel, Carol, but we just can't do it.
CAROL	How about a smaller test campaign?
AL	If you can do something for under $10,000, you can go ahead and try it.
CAROL	For $10,000 I couldn't get a large enough sampling for accurate results, what with the cost of design and printing and all. The minimum we can do it for is $20,000.

AL	I can't go for that much.
CAROL	If I cut some corners I might be able to get it down to $15,000.
AL	All right, but not a penny over $15,000.
CAROL	Thanks, Al.

Linda is the only woman on a staff team of five people. When the boss ordered an automatic coffee-maker six months ago, Linda fell into the role of coffee-maker, cleaner-upper, etc. She has decided that she doesn't want to do this any more. She calls her four colleagues into her office and says:

LINDA	I'm tired of making the coffee every morning and cleaning up after you guys. Someone else can do it from now on.
GEORGE	But you make great coffee, Linda!
LINDA	Flattery will get you nowhere, George. I'm not doing it any more, and that's all there is to it.
KEN	What's the big deal? It can't take you more than ten minutes a day.
LINDA	If it's no big deal, why don't you do it, Ken?
PHIL	Yeah, Ken, you're a bachelor—you must know how to make coffee.
BERT	Look, I think Linda's right. There's no reason she should make the coffee just because she's a woman. Why don't we share it—each of us handle it one day a week?
KEN	That's O.K. by me.
GEORGE	I'll agree if Linda will teach us all how to make it the way *she* does.
PHIL	Fine by me. Linda?
LINDA	It's a deal.

A feminist might argue that Linda got a raw deal here. After all, she made the coffee for six months, so the four guys should each have to do it for six months in order to be "fair." In the first place, life isn't necessarily fair. In the second place, Linda felt good about the compromise she made, and that's what counts.

How to Compromise:

1. First, state your wants clearly:
   I WANT YOU TO . . . or I WANT . . .
2. Persist in your original demand until you feel you are past the other person's excuses and/or his manipulative counterargument.
3. When you feel you've hit the bottom line, it's O.K. to suggest a workable compromise, or to accept the other person's compromise.
4. If your self-respect is in question, or if for any other reason you feel you can't accept the compromise—then don't. Offer what you *can* accept, but only if you are willing to take the consequences of a standoff (no agreement).
5. If you can't think on your feet, go back later, after you've had a chance to think things through, and renegotiate. You may want to say, right in the initial negotiation: "I need time to think. I'll get back to you later."
6. You don't have to make the "best deal" or a "fair deal." As long as you make a deal you can live with—well, no one ever promised that you'd always get your way. And a deal you're comfortable with is better than battling every inch of the way and ending up with an ulcer.

Some of the dialogues may have given you the impression that assertive people are tactless and repetitious. Not so. To present our points, we've sketched in the mere outlines of sample conversations. In reality, situations with potential for conflict often are somewhat more drawn out.

What counts is your approach to the circumstances you find yourself in. One of the keys to being assertive without being rude has to do with the manner in which you say things. If you speak in a friendly, pleasant, moderate tone of voice, people will not think you ill-mannered. Of course the words are vital—but they are not delivered in a vacuum.

76

A woman came up to Eileen Benson after a lecture and said, "I tried what you talked about in your last lecture and I got fired." When the woman described the incident, it turned out that she had been extremely aggressive and obnoxious toward her boss, demanding things in a sarcastic, angry tone of voice. That's not the assertive way. Aggression is not assertiveness.

HANDLING CRITICISM BY AGREEING WITH THE TRUTH IN IT

The typical nonassertive reaction to criticism of any sort is to become defensive, jump to conclusions, and feel bad. When someone says to you, "Your desk is a mess!" you jump to the conclusion that people shouldn't have messy desks, and that if you have a messy desk, you must be a mess, too.

You may respond, "I was just about to straighten it up." Or become aggressive with, "So what? It's none of your business how I keep my desk!" Or, "That's the way I work best." In any case, you're wasting important emotional energy trying to justify the messy desk to your critic.

But why jump to conclusions? And why assume it's *wrong* to have a messy desk? Why not respond calmly and coolly: "You're right. It certainly is." If your critic is trying to bug you, this will take the wind out of his sails. If he tries to escalate his criticism, you can continue:

> CRITIC   You must have a lot of fun trying to find things in that mess.
> YOU   Sometimes I do.
> CRITIC   With that junk all over your desk, how can you get any work done?
> YOU   It is a challenge.
> CRITIC   How can you stand it?
> YOU   I wonder myself, sometimes.

The important thing is this: Respond only to what the critic *says,* not what you think he's *implying.* Chances are, there is some piece of truth in it you can agree with.

77

The techniques described here for deflecting non-constructive criticism should be used only after you have tried open, straightforward communication and met with no success:

> "Mark, I really don't like it when you criticize me like this. I'd appreciate it if you'd stop doing it."

But when people—for whatever neurotic reason—use criticism to manipulate you or put you down, openness probably won't work with them. They are getting their kicks out of making you squirm. As long as you squirm, they'll keep on doing it.

Many of our new students doubt the efficacy of the criticism-deflecting techniques described here. They think it's terrible to agree with the critic in any way, shape, or form. But the point is to stop yourself from being defensive. And the critic gets to realize that you don't really care what he says about you. In other words, you're not squirming.

Students who have tried this technique with manipulative critics report that it works—and works well. And it works in personal relationships, too—even close ones. When you're no longer defending yourself against your parent's or spouse's or lover's criticism of you, the relationship takes on a different tone.

Let's look at some conversations between co-workers to see how this method for handling criticism works:

JERRY   You really bombed at the meeting this morning, Tom.

TOM   I'm sure I made some remarks that weren't 100 percent on target.

JERRY   *Some* remarks! Did you see the look on J.P.'s face? You really blew it this time!

TOM   Perhaps J.P. wasn't as thrilled as she could have been with my remarks.

JERRY   You're not kidding! I bet she takes you off the MotoRooter account for that!

TOM   It's possible that she could take me off the MotoRooter account.

JERRY	Well, doesn't that make you mad? You worked hard to get that account!
TOM	I have worked hard to get that account. It will probably bother me if J.P. takes me off it.

One of the most important benefits of this technique is that you stop feeling hurt and defensive. When you're agreeing with the truth in the critic's statement in a matter-of-fact way, it's very difficult to feel deeply hurt. You'll find yourself not caring so much about what that person says. In fact, you'll begin to see that the problem with the frequent critic is his, not yours. Whether it's some need for attention, some feeling of inferiority or superiority, or whatever, there's something bugging critical people that makes them criticize others. Once you accept the problem as theirs, instead of feeling guilty or angry, you'll find you can let it roll off your back much more easily.

BILL	You haven't worn anything but pant-suits since you came here.
SHARON	That's true, I haven't.
BILL	When a woman refuses to wear a dress, I say it's because she has ugly legs.
SHARON	I'm sure you do.
BILL	So you've got ugly legs, huh?
SHARON	Like your face, they probably wouldn't win any beauty contest.

Since this guy is terribly obnoxious, Sharon, with the same conversational tone of voice, sticks in a sarcastic zinger at the end. At this point Bill can either get angry and walk off or laugh and change the subject.

GEORGE	Harry, you're wearing a striped shirt and checked pants!
HARRY	You're right.
GEORGE	It makes me dizzy looking at you!
HARRY	I guess it does.
GEORGE	Don't you know that you're not supposed to wear stripes and checks together?

HARRY	No, I didn't know that.
GEORGE	Harry, you have no sense of *style*.
HARRY	I'm sure I don't have your sense of style, George.
GEORGE	You don't even seem to have enough sense to be bothered by it, either.
HARRY	That's true. I'm not bothered by it.
GEORGE	With your height, you should pay attention to style. Short guys like you look terrible if they don't dress right.
HARRY	I probably should pay more attention, George.

We've drawn this conversation on longer than it probably would go, just to show you how Harry can keep it up. After the first few remarks, however, George would probably become frustrated and quit. As long as Harry remains calm and unbothered, there's no percentage in George's continuing.

LINDA	You left your typewriter on all night, Carol.
CAROL	Oops—what a dumb mistake.
LINDA	That's the second time you've done that this month.
CAROL	That's true. Did you turn it off when you came in?
LINDA	Yes, but it's still hot. That wears out the motor, you know.
CAROL	I'm sure it does.
LINDA	I wish you wouldn't be so careless!
CAROL	So do I.

The important thing is for Carol to remain calm. She accepts *responsibility* for her mistake, but deflects the *guilt* that Linda is trying to dump on her.

Once you realize you don't have to be *perfect,* and that you don't have to defend yourself against every critical remark someone makes, you can relax and admit the mistakes you do make. After all, the important thing is to try and avoid them the next time, not grovel in the dirt or deny responsibility.

80

And it doesn't matter what the score is, either. You don't have to try to match up to Mr. or Ms. Perfect who sits in the next office. (Actually, they probably goof up as much as you do, but nobody watches them as closely as they watch others.) Once they see there's no percentage in watching over you like a hawk, they'll probably ease off on you. They'll get tired of criticizing you if they see they can't get to you anymore.

JIM	You're too easy on your subordinates, Stan.
STAN	It must look that way to you, Jim.
JIM	It doesn't only *look* that way to me! You let them get away with murder!
STAN	What—have you found a corpse?
JIM	I'm not kidding, Stan. You let them talk too much on the job and have their own way too much in general.
STAN	I do let them talk when it doesn't interfere with the job, that's true.
JIM	How can they respect authority when you don't act authoritative?
STAN	I guess it won't be easy for them.
JIM	You don't even care if they walk all over you!
STAN	It must look that way. But I think I'd complain if they stepped on any vital parts.
JIM	You're not taking this seriously!
STAN	I admit it. I'm not.

Humor is a great weapon for deflecting criticism because it defeats the critic's purpose: to make you feel guilty. If you're laughing, how can you be feeling guilty? They're likely to feel you're a hopeless case and give up on you.

How to Deflect Criticism:

1. Agree with the truth or generalities in the critic's statement: "It's true, my hair is a different color today."

2. Respond only to the actual *words* the critic says, not what is implied.
3. Remember that no one can make you feel inferior unless you let them.
4. Respond in a calm, conversational, matter-of-fact way.
5. Don't defend yourself or attack the other person.
6. If you made a mistake, accept the *fact,* but not *guilt* for it: "I shouldn't have left the top off the bottle."
7. If you want to apologize for a mistake, keep it a simple "I'm sorry," and leave it at that. Don't make a case out of it. We all know people who are too eager to take a lot of blame: "Oh, my god, I'm sorry! I didn't realize what I was doing! Oh, what trouble I must have caused you. If only I had thought . . ."

When the Critic's Opinion Matters

Deflecting criticism is all well and good if the critic is someone whose opinions you don't care about. But what if your boss criticizes you? How can you let it roll off your back if you're criticized by someone whose opinion matters to you?

First of all, the fact that your boss criticizes you does not mean the sky is falling. Critical feedback from superiors can be *useful information.*

The trouble is, most people are usually so wrapped up in worrying about being criticized that they miss the opportunity to find out what's going on. They apologize and hang their heads and walk away not really knowing what they did wrong, or how to correct it—or even how much or how little it means to the boss. Sometimes they end up with vague feelings of inadequacy; this only serves to make them more hesitant to show the boss their next project or idea.

The trick to turning criticism into something you can use is to *ASK FOR FEEDBACK*. Here's how it works:

> **J.P.** Tom, I'm turning the MotoRooter account over to Sidney.

Tom	I'm sorry to hear that, J.P. Why are you taking the account away from me?
J.P.	You just haven't got the right style for MotoRooter.
Tom	What is it about my style that's wrong for MotoRooter?
J.P.	You come on too strong with their purchasing agent, Harold Fusspot.
Tom	What have I said to Harold that he didn't like?
J.P.	You told him he was throwing money away by ordering flexotips in small quantities.
Tom	Did Harold feel I was wrong when I gave him that advice?
J.P.	No. He said you were right. But he didn't like the way you told him. He said you acted too damn superior.
Tom	Then if I hadn't acted so cocky about it, he might have been glad to get the advice?
J.P.	That's right.
Tom	I'd like to have another crack at Harold. I'm ready to apologize for my previous manner and talk to him more tactfully in the future.
J.P.	Well, I guess there's no harm in giving you one more try.

The main thing is to keep delving for the real reason behind the criticism. Then you'll have something solid to work on. What did the boss mean when she said Tom didn't have the right "style"? If Tom had left it at that, he wouldn't have gotten his second chance with the account and he might have come to some conclusion about his style that was entirely irrelevant to the situation. Furthermore, by digging, he found out something that might be of value to him in other situations —his possible effect on people.

Boss	Sandra, I'm sorry to have to turn you down for this promotion, but we just don't feel you're ready yet.

SANDRA	Gee, I'm really disappointed. In what way do you feel I'm not ready?
BOSS	Well, you just don't project a professional enough image.
SANDRA	I'm not sure I understand exactly what you mean. Could you explain it more?
BOSS	Well, you're young and good-looking . . . but you have . . . well . . . a little-girl look about you. It's very charming, really, but it just doesn't instill confidence in a client.
SANDRA	I look too young?
BOSS	Yes, that's it.
SANDRA	But what is it about looking young that isn't professional?
BOSS	Well, it's not just looking young. It's . . . well, compare yourself and Betty Ronson, for example.
SANDRA	She's only a couple of years older than I am.
BOSS	That's right, but she comes across as a real professional. Someone who means business.
SANDRA	Hmmmm. Is it the way I dress that's the problem?
BOSS	Yes, that's the main thing. As I said before, it's very charming and attractive . . . but for business . . .
SANDRA	If I wore tailored suits like Betty Ronson, do you think I'd look professional enough?
BOSS	That . . . and changing your hair. Pigtails just don't lend themselves to a professional image.
SANDRA	Oh, I can certainly understand that. Is there anything else?
BOSS	No—as long as you get shoes to match the tailored suits, and a more conservative hair style, that should do it.
SANDRA	You're sure?
BOSS	Yes.
SANDRA	How about giving me a couple of weeks to prove I can look the part?

	Could I have another crack at the promotion then?
Boss	You've got a deal.

This could have been a sticky situation, because people often become defensive when you discuss personal things like their manner of dress, hair style, etc. That's why the boss was reluctant to tell Sandra she wasn't dressing properly for the job. But without this information, Sandra would never know why she didn't get the promotion; she'd have some vague concept of "professional image."

By not becoming defensive or angry, Sandra was able to coax useful, specific feedback out of her boss. If she had instead started to argue with the boss, saying that image has nothing to do with ability and talent, what would she have gained? A big zero; instead, she did herself a big favor.

Note that Sandra was the one who actually brought up the dress issue: "Is it the way I dress that's the problem?" When the critic is reluctant to tell you what's really bothering him, you may have to prompt him, suggesting alternatives until you hit the right one.

John	I was wondering why I got such a small raise this year, Mr. Jennings.
Jennings	We give out raises on the basis of merit around here, John.
John	Does that mean you feel I didn't merit a larger raise?
Jennings	That's right.
John	What is it about my work that isn't meritorious, Mr. Jennings?
Jennings	When I walk through the offices, I like to see my people hard at work, John.
John	You feel I didn't work hard enough?
Jennings	That's right.
John	I don't understand. I've landed more new accounts than any of my predecessors. What is it about what I'm doing that makes you feel I'm not working hard enough?
Jennings	I'm not saying you haven't landed new

85

	accounts, John. But there's more to work than being flashy. Sitting around telling jokes and making everyone think the office is a place to gab and have fun isn't my idea of working.
JOHN	You want me to spend less time talking to people in the office?
JENNINGS	That's right. They have work to do, too, you know.
JOHN	Is that about it? I mean, is there anything else I do that bothers you?
JENNINGS	You should take your work more *seriously,* John. You act as though working is a game or a joke.
JOHN	If I cut out this kind of behavior, do you think I'll get a larger raise next year?
JENNINGS	I can't promise anything, son, but you'll certainly have a better chance for it.

John may well decide to start looking for another job on the basis of this conversation. But at least he knows where he stands and what kind of behavior Jennings wants. John can now *choose*. He can:

a) Continue his past behavior and look for another job;
b) Change his behavior and stick with Jennings; or
c) Change his behavior for reference purposes, but still look for another job.

Usually, a persistent probing will get to the bottom of a situation. But sometimes a person will simply refuse to elaborate on vague dissatisfactions, telling you nothing specific about the behavior they dislike:

CARL	Steve, I'd like to talk to you about a problem I'm having.
STEVE	Shoot. What's bothering you?
CARL	I've been here 10 months now, and I notice that I'm not getting any meatier assignments than I did my first week.
STEVE	Rome wasn't built in a day, Carl.

86

CARL	I realize that, Steve. But to tell you the truth, I think it's more than that. I've seen other people who are as new as I am getting tougher assignments. Is there something wrong with my work?
STEVE	No, there's nothing wrong with your work.
CARL	Then how come you're not giving me some meatier things?
STEVE	When I think you're ready, you'll get them.
CARL	Well, what can I do to get ready, Steve? I'd like to work on the weak areas and get to the point where I can move into some new material. What should I work on?
STEVE	Don't worry about it. You're doing O.K. You just have to be more patient.
CARL	But if I don't know what I'm doing wrong, how can I improve? Is it the way I'm writing up the reports?
STEVE	I said not to worry about it, Carl. Just keep on the way you're doing. I'll be the judge of when you're ready. I think you'd better get back to the job now.

In this case, Carl did all he could. He even prompted Steve: "Is it the way I'm writing up the reports?" But to no avail. There can be more than one explanation for such a situation. For example: Carl may be trying to move ahead too fast. Steve doesn't think there's anything wrong with his work, but just wants to move him ahead a bit more slowly. Time will tell Carl whether this is the reason.

On the other hand, it may be that Steve doesn't want Carl to move ahead, but he can't discuss it because the reason isn't legitimate (Carl has body odor, is black, young, old, the wrong religion, etc.).

In either case, Carl has let Steve know what he wants. This alone may make Steve change his behavior and start giving Carl tougher assignments. Carl should wait for a while and see what happens. If nothing changes, he might try talking to another manager about his problem. Steve may have expressed his real feelings about Carl to others, and they may give Carl the feedback he needs: "It's your bad breath, Carl!" He can start using breath spray. Or, "you're just the wrong color for this place, Carl." He can start discrimination proceedings, or look for another job.

If Carl gets no feedback from anyone, and the situation doesn't change, he definitely ought to start looking for another job.

Getting Passive People to Open Up. Asking for feedback is also a useful method for dealing with people who have a passive style of coping. They are afraid to tell you how they really feel and what they really want. Perhaps you've given them cause to be afraid of you in the past. Maybe it's because you're "the boss," or it could be their own timidity. In any case, by probing and asking for feedback, you can get to the core of the problem rather than dealing with the vague dissatisfactions they present you with. Here's an example:

RALPH   I'd like to dictate now, Marie.

MARIE   But I'm working on that rush letter you wanted out today, Ralph.

RALPH   How come you always save the rush work for late in the afternoon?

MARIE   I'm sorry.

RALPH   Every time I want to dictate to you in the afternoon, you have something else to do. Is there something about me dictating to you then that you don't like?

MARIE   I think it's better to dictate in the mornings.

RALPH   Why is that better?

MARIE   Then I have the rest of the day to type up my notes.

RALPH   But I don't expect you to finish what I dictate in the afternoons. I expect you to type it the next day. Is it that you're worried about reading your notes the next day?

MARIE	No, I don't have any trouble reading them the next day.
RALPH	Well, there's something about dictating in the afternoons that you don't like. What is it?
MARIE	Well, when you start dictating, you lose track of the time.
RALPH	Oh! You're afraid I'll dictate past quitting time?
MARIE	Yes. If I don't catch the 5:15 bus, I have to stand all the way home.
RALPH	I can understand how you feel . . . I wouldn't want that to happen to me, either. So how about if you remind me, whenever we're dictating late in the afternoon, to stop at exactly five minutes to five? When you say it's time, we'll quit, even if we're in the middle of a letter. How would that be?
MARIE	That sounds fine.

The first few times Ralph had dictated late in the afternoon, Marie had missed her bus. From then on she always tried to be busy in the afternoon so Ralph wouldn't be able to dictate late. This was a passive way for her to cope with the problem. In order to find out what was behind her resistance, Ralph had to assume there was a reason behind her balking behavior. And there was. Once it came out in the open, they worked out a compromise.

Here, once again, the important thing is the attitude and tone you use. If Ralph had spoken in a sarcastic or accusing tone, Marie probably would not have been able to admit the real reason she wasn't available for dictation late in the afternoon. But she sensed that Ralph was genuinely interested in the problem. And he was persistent. So Marie overcame her reticence. The work-flow problem was solved, and the anticipatory anxiety Marie felt many afternoons disappeared. It takes a sympathetic approach—concern for the other person's point of view and feelings.

Here's another example:

It is the practice of department heads in Betty's

company to have an informal meeting every so often to bring each other up to date. Roger, one of the other department heads, never does this—he goes individually to the other department heads when he has something to tell them. But he always leaves Betty out. She wants to find out why and what can be done about it:

BETTY   Roger, I feel left out because you never let me know what's going on in your department. You haven't called a meeting since last year.

ROGER   I just haven't found it necessary, Betty.

BETTY   But you've held individual meetings with other department heads. I feel I'm being particularly avoided. Is it because I'm a woman?

ROGER   Of course not!

BETTY   Well, what is it, then? I know I must be doing something to bug you.

ROGER   If you want to know what's going on in my department, I'll send you a report, O.K.?

BETTY   But why don't you want to tell me in person? What's wrong with having a general meeting, the way everybody else does?

ROGER   I like to do it my way.

BETTY   But I understand that before I came, you used to hold meetings just like everyone else does. So it must have something to do with me. I'd like to clear this up between us, Roger. If you tell me what it is, maybe I can change.

ROGER   O.K., Betty. If you want the truth, here it is. I don't care to be shot down in front of everybody the way you've done to Stan and Jim in the past!

BETTY   Gee, I did that?

ROGER   You interrogated them as though they were on trial, and made them look foolish in front of the rest of us.

BETTY   I didn't realize asking all those ques-

	tions would seem like interrogation. I just wanted to know more about things, since I was new and all. So you thought I would do the same to you?
ROGER	That's right.
BETTY	Listen, Roger, I appreciate finding this out. I probably antagonized a few other people, too.
ROGER	You sure did.
BETTY	Listen, if I shape up at the next meeting, will you give me another chance?
ROGER	Sure. And I'm sorry I came down so hard on you. I never thought that you didn't realize what you were doing. I guess one of us should have told you right in the beginning.
BETTY	Well, next time I hope you will.
ROGER	Sure thing.

Very often, people in an organization will complain about somebody to each other, but not directly to the person. This makes it very difficult for the one involved to figure out why he or she is being snubbed.

People expect others to read their minds. Roger and the rest of the group probably thought: "Betty should know enough to shut up in front of the group and approach us later if she wants to know something." But no one told her. If Roger hadn't refused to hold any more meetings, Betty might never have realized how obnoxious her behavior was to the group.

This happens a lot. People think someone is acting deliberately vicious, intending to hurt them, when he or she isn't aware of the impact of his actions. If they don't tell him, how can they expect him to change?

Communication among humans is very complex. It's something we have to work on constantly, because we are always assuming things, or covering up our feelings, or expecting people to know what we want without our telling them. We all could be mind-readers if everybody had the same values, the same likes and dislikes. But we don't. You may not like it if somebody puts his feet up on a desk when talking with you; another person may be oblivious to it. So only by constant work—probing for people's real feelings, trying to be aware of subtle signals from others, getting in touch with our *own* feelings and expressing them directly—can we hope to make our relationships work.

And that's what management is: a series of working relationships with peers, subordinates, superiors, customers, and clients. If communications are blocked, it becomes all the more difficult to accomplish our goals.

Sure, you manage to fumble through. You give orders, and take orders, and work gets done. But every time communication is blocked, and resentment, anxiety, fear, or anger is felt, work is impeded. Because you're human, you can't help but let your emotions interfere with your actions.

If you care about getting the job done, then clear, reasonable, honest communications are the best approach. The results of poor communications can range from simple misunderstanding of a single statement to a total rejection and hatred of the individual.

People are clever. They can devise all sorts of mutinies that cannot be detected. Things will get all fouled up—and you'll never know why.

Anxiety. One very good clue that something is rotten in the communications area is a feeling of anxiety. If you get this feeling after walking out of the boss's office, for example, review in your mind what was discussed and find the thing that's bugging you. Something was not clear, either in what the boss said or in the way you reacted. Perhaps you didn't say what you really thought about something. Maybe you felt he was displeased with you in some way, but you didn't get the necessary feedback to do something about it.

Whatever it is, whenever you feel this anxiety, try to pin down the specific cause—and then try to do something about it. Go back in and talk to the boss again. Tell him how you feel (once you've pinpointed the particular problem). Get it settled; don't let it continue to gnaw away at you.

You may gnaw have a feeling of anxiety whenever you deal with a particular person. What is it about these encounters that makes you feel this way? Do you feel that the person is manipulating you? Does he or she put you on the defensive? Pick apart your last conversation with him until you figure out what it is that's bugging you.

Celia was always anxious with a co-worker, Rod, if other people were present. Rod had the habit of putting an arm around women, sometimes kissing them. Whenever he did this to Celia, she became embarrassed and red in the face. His behavior upset her very much, but she was afraid that if she told him to stop it, she would hurt his feelings and destroy the relationship that they had, which basically was a good one.

Finally Celia got up the courage to talk to Rod when they were alone and tell him that his behavior embarrassed her. He said he was sorry he had upset her and would not do it in the future. And he kept his word.

When facing the person who's causing you the anxiety, be specific about the behavior you want changed. And don't assume evil motives on the other person's part. Suppose Celia had spoken to Rod this way:

"Rod, I'm not your personal property and you have no right to kiss me and put your arm around me! I'm warning you—the next time you try it you're going to get a swift kick where it hurts!"

Here Celia is blaming Rod not only for the physical gestures, but also for an attitude he might never have had: treating her as if she were his personal property. After an attack like that it would be difficult for Rod to remain friendly to her.

Here's an assertive way to handle the situation:

CELIA   Rod, I have a problem. When you kiss me or put an arm around me in public, I get embarrassed.

ROD   But I don't mean anything by it, Celia. I do it because I like you, and that's just how I treat women I like.

CELIA   I understand that, Rod, and I'm glad you like me. I like you, too. But I can't help blushing and getting embarrassed, so I'd like you to stop doing it.

93

ROD   Sure . . . I don't want to hurt you. If I slip in the future, kick me or something, O.K.?

CELIA   O.K.

In this instance, Celia starts out by saying *she* has a problem. Rather than blaming Rod, or imputing any motive to his behavior, she simply asks him to stop the behavior because of *her* feelings about it. Thus she hasn't attacked him, and because he wasn't under attack he was readily able to react in an open, receptive manner instead of becoming defensive.

How to Turn Criticism Into Useful Feedback:

1. When there is vague criticism, probe to find out specifically what you're doing wrong:
   "What is it about my work that's second-rate, sir?"
2. Keep probing until the critic comes up with the real reasons for the dissatisfaction.
3. If you can't seem to elicit it, do some prompting:
   "Is it my leaving five minutes early every day that disturbs you?"
4. No matter what the person says, don't act defensive or hurt. The criticism may be useful information that can help you do a better job in the future. Think of it that way.
5. Ask how you can change to improve and meet the person's requirements in the future.
6. When trying to get feedback from a passive, timid person, remember to remain sympathetic and keep any sarcasm or accusations out of your messages.

Handling Complaints or Criticism From Clients and Customers

This is a delicate situation because you *do* care how your customer or client feels. If he's angry or upset, you want to help him "discharge" these feelings—i.e., get them off his chest. That in itself will usually make him feel better. You also want to find out what the problem is and solve it as quickly as possible.

So the first thing to do in dealing with an irate customer is to let him know you empathize with his feelings and understand his problem. The second thing is to assure him that you will do everything possible to help him.

Take this telephone conversation as an example:

MANAGER   Can I help you?

CUSTOMER   [angrily] I paid my bill two weeks ago, and now I've just gotten a dunning letter from you! What kind of an outfit are you running there?

MANAGER   I'm really sorry, sir. I'd be angry if that happened to me, too.

CUSTOMER   You're damn right! How can you let such a thing happen?

MANAGER   We must have made a mistake, sir, unless your check was lost in the mail.

CUSTOMER   Well, it wasn't lost in the mail because I got my cancelled check back from my bank.

MANAGER   Then we must have goofed. Would you please give me your name so I can have things straightened out?

CUSTOMER   O.K. [now he has calmed down]

The objective here is to defuse the customer's anger by empathizing with him: "I'd be angry if that happened to me, too." The manager also admitted right away that a mistake had been made. Finally, by asking for the customer's name he showed that he was actually taking steps to straighten out the error.

Here's another situation:

CUSTOMER   You sold me a lemon!

MANAGER   What's the matter, Mr. Sloan?

CUSTOMER   Everything's the matter! I didn't even get the car home before the battery conked out, the door handle fell off, and I got two flat tires!

MANAGER   Wow! I can understand how you feel! That's terrible!

CUSTOMER   It sure is, and on top of that your

	salesman tells me it's too late to do anything about it tonight! What am I supposed to use for transportation?
MANAGER	I don't blame you for being upset, Mr. Sloan. We should have checked the car more carefully before we let you take it out. I'm sorry about that.
CUSTOMER	What are you going to do about it?
MANAGER	The servicemen have left for the day, but I'll see that everything's taken care of first thing in the morning.
CUSTOMER	But how am I supposed to get home tonight?
MANAGER	I'll have Jerry drive you home right now, O.K.?
CUSTOMER	Thanks, I appreciate it.

The manager sympathized with the customer, agreed that a mistake had been made, and offered to do what he could to help. The customer knows he can't get his car fixed at eight o'clock at night, but he's angry. To start arguing with him would only make him angrier and more unreasonable. By dissipating the anger first, a workable compromise is possible.

To Handle Customers' Complaints or Criticism:

1. Listen to the problem, asking questions as necessary to find out exactly what's bugging them.
2. Sympathize with their angry or upset feelings: "I'd be mad, too."
3. Show them that you understand their problem.
4. Admit it readily if you or your organization made a mistake.
5. *After* they've had a chance to express their feelings, offer to do the best thing possible to solve their problem.
6. If you can't help them, or not in the manner they desire, let them know you're sorry about it. If possible, explain why you can't help them:
   "I'm sorry we can't fix your car tonight, because all the servicemen have left for the day."

7. Take whatever steps are necessary to make sure the problem doesn't occur again.

The Benefits of Assertive Communication. When you start talking to people on the basis of the actual words they use, instead of on what you *think* they *might* be saying, you'll be encouraging more open communication. You'll be forcing people to say what they mean, to spell it out.

Whatever you do, don't try to guess. If you're not sure what someone meant, ask him. Phrase in simple terms what you think they meant: "Do you mean . . ."

Whenever someone uses highfalutin' language, ask him or her what he is talking about. Translate what he says into plain terms. If he says: "Don't you know what obfuscation means?" say, "No, I'm not sure I do. Could you tell me what you mean by it?"

Straightforward, assertive talking may irritate some people at first. If they've been able to manipulate you in the past, they may resent the fact they can no longer do this. If you start asking for the things you want, they may worry about their ability to say "No" to you.

But in the long run you'll find people enjoying you more when you're assertive, because they now know where you stand. They don't have to second-guess you anymore. They don't have to worry whether they've hurt your feelings, because they know you'll tell them if they do. That will encourage *them* to act assertively, too, creating a better environment all around.

The Practice

section one

ASSERTIVE SUPERVISION

"Few things help an individual more than to place responsibility upon him and to let him know that you trust him."

— *Booker T. Washington*

One of the reasons employees join unions is that they want to have some degree of control of their situation. They want to know that they have the "right" to so many sick days or so much vacation time. They don't want to have to depend on a benevolent organization to give it to them.

People have a basic desire for power and control over their own lives. So many things are beyond our control—weather, the economy, accidents, health, war. Sometimes it seems that we are merely being blown about by circumstance, with no control over what befalls us.

But this is a passive, defeatist attitude. There is *much* we can do to control what happens to us. Even such things as sickness and accidents can be influenced by our attitudes and actions.

In order to put food on the table, we must work. But the fact that we *must* work doesn't mean we can't find satisfaction in it. Quite the opposite: Work can be one of the most rewarding things in our lives.

But it can't be rewarding if we feel powerless and at the mercy of our superiors. If we are merely putting in time, not growing or stretching our capacities, work can be a drudge.

In and of itself, doing any task well can be satisfying. The kind of work that challenges and stimulates each of us will of course vary from individual to individual. But once a person has found the work that suits him or her, he should then be left alone to do it.

We don't mean he should be ignored. But he shouldn't be hampered by unnecessary restrictions, rules, requirements, and aggravations. He should be given as much control over his own work and work environment as possible.

A manager told us recently about a problem he was having with his part-time home business. He had hired high-school kids to do various clerical tasks for him. One girl in particular worked very fast when he gave her a big pile of work to do. But on days when he gave her a short task, and then another task when she was finished with the first, and so on, she seemed to work much more slowly. She also acted annoyed when he brought out another batch after she thought she was finished.

The problem was simple. She wanted to know how much work she would have to do in a particular period of time. She didn't like having the work doled out in bits and pieces. She wanted to see the whole picture and set up her own work schedule. Psychological "set," based on expectations, is very important. For example, if you know that you have to work three hours overtime one night, you don't start letting down just before your usual quitting time. But if you expect to leave at the regular time and your boss comes to you at the last minute with a three-hour task—it can be a bit of a jolt, can't it?

A similar situation occurred in a pharmaceutical company's sales department. Marie, a young woman, was being trained to replace the head of statistical information. She was bright, fast, mature, and eager to learn the job. But the older woman she was replacing refused to let the younger one get a real grip on what the position entailed; instead, she gave the work out piecemeal with little explanation as to how the pieces fit into the larger picture. Marie had to come to this woman every few hours for a new batch of work. The woman wouldn't be retiring for almost a year—and so Marie quit. A good worker was lost.

In general, people like to plan their own work, set their own schedules, and make as many of the decisions concerning their labors as possible. They also like to be in control of their own work area, desk, tools, etc. The more you can allow individual control over these things, the better.

Training and Development. Giving an employee control over his work is not the same as dumping a job on him that he has no idea how to do. Just picture an employee, especially a new one, sitting at his work station overwhelmed by a mass of work he can't make head or tail of, while the supervisor walks away saying, "Call me if you have any problems." The poor worker feels like yelling at his boss's quickly departing back: "Wait! I've got one! Where do I start?"

You may be saying to yourself, "Aha, that's not *my* problem! We've got a whole training department that orients and trains new people before I even see them. We've got the most sophisticated audio-visual, pro-grammed-instruction, classroom and on-the-job training systems on the market. Personnel won't let one of my people stay at his desk for two consecutive weeks without dragging him out to some new kind of training session. If anything, my people are *over*-trained!"

Don't kid yourself. No matter how much training your subordinates receive, you've still got to set the style in your own department. Do you take the sink-or-swim attitude (the employee better know what he's doing, or figure it out on his own!)? Or do you take the opposite approach and encourage your employees to clear with you before they attempt anything? In the first case you'll end up with subordinates spending a lot of time sweating out a tough decision or plunging in with the wrong move. In the latter case, you won't get anything done yourself because you'll be spending all your time coddling your staff. With proper job training you can avoid both these extremes.

Tell Your Employees What You Expect. The more clearly you communicate to your subordinates what you expect from them, the more likely they'll be to fulfill your requirements. For example, if you like to see ideas only after they've been developed into full-blown, detailed proposals, tell your employees this. If you want to hear about something in its initial idea stage, before it's fully developed, let them know this is what you want. The more specific information you can give your subordinates about your preferences, the easier it will be for them to conform to your wishes.

Managers often expect subordinates to somehow know or guess what's expected of them. Joe had a subordinate who came in five to twenty minutes late every day. Joe couldn't understand this. "What's wrong with that guy?" he said to himself. "Is he deliberately trying to get my goat?" Joe found himself getting angrier and angrier with this otherwise very competent worker. At review time, Joe gave him a low rating, and the worker asked why. When Joe confronted him with his lateness, the man was truly surprised. He hadn't realized punctuality was that important to Joe. He figured that since he always got his work done, no one would care if he was a few minutes late. One word from Joe initially would have saved them both a lot—Joe his wasted anger and frustration, the worker his low merit rating.

No matter how universal you believe your standards to be, don't ever assume a subordinate is aware of them. Tell new employees what kind of behavior you expect from them. Of course, you may not cover every base initially. How were you to know the guy was going to bring his pet hamster to work with him? Should you have thought ahead and said to every new worker, "No pet hamsters allowed on the job"?

That's What Feedback Is For. You can't think of everything. So when something comes up that you didn't explain initially, tell your subordinate about it. And tell him or her right away. This doesn't mean you have to give a warning notice the first time somebody comes in late, takes a half hour too long for lunch, insults a customer, or is rude to your boss. The important thing is whether the employee intends to do better next time—and whether there was awareness of having erred.

In other words, if Kathy insults a customer and has no idea this is undesirable behavior, then tell her right away. But if it was a slip because the customer espe-

101

cially aggravated her and she was under a lot of pressure that day, there may be no need to say anything. Kathy will probably censure herself. With an old employee, you know if it's out of character for him or her to react like that. If it's a newer worker, keep an eye open to see if it happens again.

How To Say It. *How* you give employees feedback on their behavior is crucial. Here are some examples of how *not* to say it:

1. "Ursula, if you ever do that again, you're fired!"
2. "Larry, how could a bright guy like you do such a stupid thing?"
3. "Bennie, if you'd read the company policy book, you'd know you can't do that."
4. "If Ms. Jones catches you doing that, you'll be in real trouble!"
5. "Cynthia, don't you think it would be easier if you did it this way?"
6. "George, I don't like to say anything, but I think maybe you might be doing that wrong."

What's bad about the above statements? Number 1 is threatening, designed to make Ursula hate you, fear you, or both. Number 2 puts Larry down in such a way that there's not much he can do to maintain his self-respect in front of you and still admit he made a mistake (unless, of course, he uses assertive methods of coping with your criticism).

Number 3 puts the responsibility on the rule book instead of on you. *You're* in charge, and *you* want the worker to change his behavior—so you must take the responsibility for that message.

Number 4 is nothing but a threat; it doesn't explain or have any other constructive characteristics. In Number 5 you've added a question, and you might very well get this response: "No, I think it's easier to do it this way." And Number 6 is weak and wishy-washy. If you don't like to say anything, don't say it. But if you have some constructive criticism you *do* want to give, give it.

Here's how the above statements might be improved:

1. "Ursula, I'm very upset with you for calling Mr. Smith a male chauvinist pig. I feel you've jeopardized one of our biggest accounts and I'm concerned that something like this might happen again. Do you have any ideas on how we can solve this conflict between you and Smith?"

2. "Larry, I'd like you to recompute these figures. Column 3 should be added to, not subtracted from, column 4. Here's the reason . . ."

3. "Bennie, I can't let you work today unless you go home and put on some shoes. It's against company policy to work in bare feet because it's considered unsafe."

4. "Ted, I'm not your supervisor, but I notice that you're putting the red balls into the blue boxes and the blue balls into the red boxes. I thing Ms. Jones wants the red balls put into the red boxes and the blue balls put into the blue boxes."

5. "Cynthia, I want you to try pulling this lever down with both hands, because I think it will be easier that way. Let me show you . . ."

6. "George, the machine won't work when you put the paper in that way. Please turn it around before you insert it."

Note how these responses state directly what is wanted and put the responsibility where it belongs: on you, the manager. In Number 3, you make it clear that you intend to uphold the company rule about bare feet, and you also explain the reason for the rule.

In Number 4, the important thing is to have the proper attitude and tone of voice. If you treat the situation as if you're giving Ted a helpful tip, he's less likely to resent your interference.

You Need to Know Clearly What You Want in Order to Give Subordinates a Clear Message. Do you sometimes give out assignments with no clearly defined goals, hoping your subordinates will somehow get the right vibes and come up with something workable? Do you tolerate a certain kind of behavior in one worker but not in another? Do you have different standards on different days, depending on how heavy traffic was that morning? You can't communicate what you want to your employees if your goals and standards are vague or changeable.

While it's not always easy, it's important for a manager to be as consistent as possible in his expectations of employees. If you accept a late report without comment one month and become furious about it another, your employees are likely to end up confused and resentful. Also be consistent from employee to employee: Hold the same standards for one as for another. Playing favorites can create all kinds of havoc.

You may not even be aware of your inconsistencies. This is why it's important to put your standards and goals in writing. You will sharpen your thoughts, and you will be more aware. Exactly what behavior is important to you? What's the highest percentage of error permissible—or that you can tolerate—on a project? Exactly how do you want your secretary to handle callers when you're in conference? Is it important to you that your salespeople dress conservatively? Don't ignore what's important to you, no matter how trivial, because it will affect your attitude toward your subordinates. How is John to know you can't stand him wearing blue jeans to visit clients if you never tell him? Perhaps he *should* know—but if you tell him, he *knows*.

Two-Way Communication. The trick to effective training is progressive two-way communication. You tell the employee something. Then you ask him to tell you what you said. If he can repeat it back to you, that's a start. Just a start. Giving you back your own words may have no connection to his having understood them.

Whenever possible, you should not only *tell* him what to do, but *show* him. Let him see how *you* handle a tough customer on the phone. When you're sure he understands the what and the how, let him try it. But don't go away. Observe him doing the task, correct and encourage him, and then observe again.

Once you've watched him doing the job correctly several times, then you can leave him on his own. But not for long if the tasks are complex. In those cases, return several times, gradually granting him more freedom, until he's fully weaned.

Ask Questions. When you're training a new employee, ask *lots* of questions:

"Do you understand what I said?"
"How would you rephrase it in your own words?"
"What do you think should be changed in this procedure?"
"What part of this don't you understand?"
"How do you think this could be done better?"

Don't stop when an employee says "Yes" after you ask him, "Do you understand what I want?" Have him tell you, in his own words, what he thinks you want. Otherwise you leave yourself wide open for a botched job and a comment such as, "Oh, I thought you meant . . ."

Encourage the Trainee to Ask Questions. Most trainees don't ask enough questions because they're afraid of looking stupid. Therefore you've got to go all out to encourage them to open up. Simply saying "Are there any questions?" isn't enough. Keep going:

"What about section one here? Do you have any questions about that? Would you like me to repeat any part of the instructions? How about putting the flap on the doodle here? Is there anything you don't understand about that? It's one of the toughest parts to understand, and most people don't get it right the first time, so I want to be sure you're clear on it. Would you like me to show it to you again?"

Once you get an employee to start asking questions, *the way you answer him will determine whether or not he'll continue to ask questions when he doesn't understand something*. If you *don't* want your employees to ask you a lot of questions, try the following responses:

"This must be the hundredth time you've asked me that question, Murkwood!"
"You really want me to answer *that?*"
"Well, like I *just said,* you take the gimcrack and . . ."

Another way to stop questions is to give employees a forty-five minute answer when a thirty-second one would have made things clear. Or to answer a simple question with jargon and five-syllable words. Some managers squelch the first question before it's even asked: They walk stiffly through the office, not smiling at anyone; look down at all underlings; never indulge in small talk with subordinates; always keep their door closed; and have a bodyguard for a secretary.

Now that we've covered how *not* to answer an employee's question, let's look at the proper way to do it. Once again, feedback is the key to effective communication. Before you attempt to answer the employee's question, make sure you know what the question is. The surest way to do this is to rephrase or state the question in your own words: "You want to know how the framble should be connected to the diverble, is that correct?" Or, "You want me to repeat the steps you should take when an item is out of stock, is that right?"

By repeating or rephrasing the question, you'll give the employee a chance to say, "No, I understand that. What I need to know is . . ." or, "Yes, that's right." Now that you have the question nailed down you can proceed with the answer.

The manner or attitude you have when answering questions is all-important. By treating the question and the questioner with respect, your answer will show that you consider both of them to be worthwhile and are eager to take the time to clear things up. A hurried response or sarcastic tone will not encourage the employee to ask more questions.

If you find that an employee asks the same question repeatedly, or that he's unable to understand your answer, try taking a new approach. Don't simply keep repeating an answer over and over. See if there's another way to explain the situation. Better yet, give an example. Or demonstrate the answer in addition to explaining it.

When a Subordinate Asks Too Many Questions. Some people are so afraid of doing something wrong that they constantly question every step of the way. They want your approval before they take any chances.

They figure that this way they won't go wrong. The problem is that that way they don't learn to be independent, and you end up spending all your time telling them what to do.

To solve this problem, just remember our basic rule: Tell your employee what you want and expect from him. Don't wait for things to build up so that one day you end up shouting, "For God's sake, Milton, figure it out for yourself for once!"

When you first notice an employee clinging to you for assurance, let him know that you want some other kind of behavior. For example:

"Milton, I know you're asking me questions because you want to do the job perfectly, but I'd rather you tried to take some steps on your own, now. I'm confident that you can handle these kinds of details yourself. Today I want you to work on this project without checking with me each step of the way. When you're finished, we'll go over it and see how you did. Of course, if anything comes up that you feel you *must* talk to me about, go ahead, but I'd like you to try to do it on your own."

You may have to wean this type of employee slowly, gradually cutting down his frequency for checking with you. Simultaneously assure him of your confidence in his ability to do the work.

Sometimes it's a superior's demand for perfection that makes a subordinate question every step before he takes it. If employees are afraid they won't be able to meet your standards, or that they'll be called down if a project isn't perfect, then they may try to avoid responsibility for the results by having you O.K. each minute detail along the way.

So check yourself out on this. Are you allowing employees room to breathe . . . to operate in their own style . . . to make an occasional error . . . to feel free to carry a project through to completion even if it doesn't come out 100 percent perfect?

Don't Forget Positive Feedback. When a new employee is beginning to perform a procedure correctly, that's the time for positive reinforcement: "You're doing a good job, Jack; keep it up." It's a constructive way to introduce criticism, too: "You've got it perfect up to this section. Now, here's how you should change it after that . . ."

But be honest and don't go overboard with your praise. If you're always telling Carol what a great job she's doing, and then give her a low evaluation come time for a raise, she won't appreciate your sweet words. Honestly point out an employee's steps forward as well as his steps backward to help keep him heading in the right direction.

Let Your Subordinates Grow. Coaching employees by telling, showing, questioning, and giving feedback on their performance is all well and good. You've told them what you expect. You've shown them how to do it. You've made sure they understand what you want, and you've observed them at work. Now it's time to loosen the reins a bit.

There's usually more than one way to get a job done effectively, and your subordinate's preferred way may not be yours. Just as you need to take responsibility for your own life and work, he needs to take responsibility for his.

As soon as he is ready, give him room to decide how his own work will be done, to set his own priorities, to find the best way to do what needs to be done.

People are different. Some will be ready when they walk in the door. They'll look over the situation and ask whatever questions are necessary for them to orient themselves to the company and the job. They'll come to you when they need help, and later on to make suggestions and expand their field of influence; these are the self-starters. To get the best work from these people —leave them alone. Don't hover over them; challenge them. Give them the hardest jobs you think they can handle. They'll love it. And by all means give them enough work to do: They hate to be idle.

Other people will need closer supervision and more extensive training. Give them the help they need, but back off as soon as you see they can handle things themselves. Be observant of their strengths and weaknesses and try to find useful outlets for their strengths. Give them training and practice to overcome the weaknesses, or try to put them in spots where the weakness won't matter.

For example, some people are good on the telephone but terrible in person-to-person exchanges. Some people are at their best moving about in the field. Others prefer a desk in a quiet office. Some are good with numbers, some good with people, some with problems. The better you can match a person to work that he's happy with and good at, the better the job that will get done, and the more satisfied your workers will be.

Let Subordinates in on the Larger Picture. Joe Smith, owner of a heating-oil company, worked for weeks and finally landed a big, new account. It meant offering 30 days' credit, but Joe wasn't worried. All new accounts went through a routine credit check by his bookkeeper.

At the end of 30 days, Joe called the account—and found that the manager had fled, absconding with the money, including what was owed to Joe's company.

What happened to the credit investigation that was supposed to have been done on this account? In processing it, the bookkeeper came upon a stumbling block —not enough information to check on. So the papers sat on her desk.

Yet Joe's bookkeeper was an excellent and conscientious worker. What had gone wrong? We suspect there were two problems. First, Joe not only should have alerted her to the big billings likely with this important new customer, but he himself should have known when to expect the credit check to come through and should have asked to see it.

Second, credit checking should not have been allowed to be a simple routine without meaning. The *reason* for credit checking should have been discussed with the bookkeeper a long time ago. (This may seem too obvious to explain, especially to a professional, but what is "obvious" to you may not be so to somebody else. The bookkeeper incident actually happened.)

How many procedures in your department are considered "routine" by employees? What would be the consequences if these routines were fouled up? Do your subordinates know how costly mistakes could be? Are they aware of alternative procedures in case things don't go as planned? Do they know what to do when something unusual comes up?

By filling them in on the larger picture, you give your people a feel for what's important. It helps them relate their piece to the whole plan. They'll be able to spot more mistakes faster, suggest changes to benefit the company's goals, and emphasize those areas of their work that are the most important.

When Subordinates Make Mistakes. The famous heart surgeon Michael DeBakey trained under Dr. Alton Ochsner of New Orleans. One day in 1938, Ochsner, with DeBakey assisting, opened a patient's rib cage before an assembly of surgeons. DeBakey retracted the aorta, but his index finger exerted a bit too much pressure and punctured the aorta. Fearing he had killed the patient, DeBakey whispered the news to Ochsner. Ochsner said calmly, "Just leave your finger there. Don't pull it out."

Ochsner sutured around the wound and then asked DeBakey to pull his finger out. "Ochsner could, at that moment, have destroyed my confidence—and my career," says DeBakey. But Ochsner treated the incident as a simple mistake. *He concentrated on the solution, not the error.*

How do you act when subordinates make mistakes? Do you blow up and humiliate them? Do you avoid mentioning errors?

Both courses are extreme—and extreme is bad. If you let mistakes go unmentioned, the subordinate may not learn the right way to do things. If your criticism is harsh, many people will be afraid to try things.

The best way to treat mistakes is matter-of-factly. Once the mistake is pointed out, the subordinate will want to correct it.

If he continues to make the same mistake, keep after him—assertively. Don't let him wear *you* down. And don't be afraid to let him know how you feel about it:

> STEVE Ron, I'd like to talk to you about your expense reports.
>
> RON Uh-oh, what did I do? Forget the back-up receipts again?

STEVE	That's right. And it means we have to hold up the report for our department, which will hold up our reimbursement check and mess up our cash-flow situation again.
RON	I'm sorry, Steve. I'll bring in the receipts tomorrow.
STEVE	Ron, you do this just about every month, and I'm pretty upset by it. What can we do to make sure it doesn't happen again?
RON	I'll take care of it.
STEVE	That's what you said last month, Ron. That's not enough for me this time.
RON	Well, what do you want me to do?
STEVE	I want you to bring in your receipts every day and record them in this folder in my office.
RON	But that's an extra trip to the office at the end of every day.
STEVE	Ron, you're a good man and I want to keep you. But I also want your receipts in on time from now on.
RON	Look, I didn't realize this was so important to you. Give me one more chance and I promise I'll take care of it right this time.
STEVE	[Recognizing that he hadn't earlier told Ron of the importance of timeliness] O.K. But if you're late next month, you start coming in every day.
RON	Don't worry—I'll do everything I can to avoid that!

If an employee continues to botch something up, a manager must ask himself this: How valuable is this subordinate to me? What am I willing to do to keep him? If a manager is willing to spend extra time and effort, as Steve was, he can usually come up with ways to help the subordinate change. If the undesirable behavior is minor, and the manager can cope with it, he may simply decide to put up with it in order to retain the employee.

111

But it's really a matter of what you can live with, and being willing to lose in order to gain. But the gain must outweigh the loss: No matter how good and valued a subordinate, if you or the company are suffering because of his refusal to change, it may be time to say goodbye. However, you should first give a warning—if the person realizes his job is at stake, he might just be motivated finally to change.

Firing a Subordinate. This is an unpleasant last resort. It should happen only after you've communicated clearly exactly what the employee is doing wrong and what he must do to correct his behavior. You should also make it clear to him that he *will* be fired if he doesn't change.

This is another area where managers often expect people to read their minds: "He's been screwing things up around here for six months—he *must* have known he was going to be fired!" Certainly, many employees are aware of this possibility, but often they are not. Why not give them the benefit of the doubt and *tell* them? If you've put up with them so far, isn't it worth one last talk to possibly turn them into a useful worker?

What also may come out of such a conversation is the realization that the employee has no intention of changing his way, that he *wants* to be fired. He probably doesn't admit it to himself, but by continuing to ignore his boss's criticism, he is asking to be let go.

Suppose the conversation between Steve and Ron had gone this way:

> STEVE Ron, you're a good man, and I'd hate to lose you. But if the receipts are late once more, that's what's going to happen. For me, there's no other alternative.
>
> RON I can't believe you'd fire me over a petty thing like that!
>
> STEVE If it's so petty, Ron, why can't you do what I want?
>
> RON Because I don't like somebody pushing me on stuff like that. If I worked for myself I wouldn't have to take this petty crap.

STEVE	Maybe that's what you really want to do?
RON	Yes, it is what I want, but I'm not ready yet.
STEVE	Then you do want to stay on here for a while?
RON	Yeah, I do—at least for six months.
STEVE	Well I'd like to have you for that six months, Ron—*if* you get those receipts in on time. Is it worth it to you?
RON	I guess it is.

When somebody continues to balk or foul things up there's usually something behind it. In Ron's case, he wanted to be working for himself. Somebody else might be suffering with a heavy load of personal problems. Another might simply be unhappy working for you and looking for an excuse to find another job. By confronting the person with the issue, you at least have a chance to find out what's going on. Isn't this better than putting up with it in silence, and then firing the person without warning one Friday afternoon?

Just such a thing occurred when a vice president of personnel hired a new director for his manpower training department. The director had great ideas and made impressive presentations. But he never got around to actually *doing* anything. This drove the V.P. crazy. But he never told his new director. Six months later, on a Friday afternoon. . .

Fear of Firing. It's hell to fire someone, especially if you start thinking about his sick mother and five hungry children. But not firing someone you know you *should* fire is an act against yourself, the other people in your department, and your company. If you think about it, you're even hurting the consumers who buy your company's products and services.

And you're doing the subordinate an injustice. By protecting him in this way, you are taking over the responsibility for his life. You are assuming he is unable to take care of himself and solve his own problems, giving him false feedback about how the world operates, distorting his sense of reality.

As for the actual act of firing, anticipation is usually

113

the worst of it. Once you get the words out, the tension will be relieved. Then the employee will walk out of your life and you won't see him or her again. Therefore, the sooner the better.

Firing will never be a happy experience. Some people hope that the employee will do something *so* bad, they'll have an excuse to feel enraged and fire him on the spot. But this is ducking the issue.

Firing people is part of a manager's job, just as promoting them is. You may suffer each time you have to do it. That's understandable. But don't let it stop you from doing what you have to do.

Groups. Two-way communication is tough enough; trying to get a group of people to communicate effectively is really a job. If working with groups is so difficult, you may wonder why you should even bother. One reason is that people generally are more committed to an idea if they have helped form it.

For example, if there's a problem and you tell your subordinates how they should solve it, they are more likely to resist than if they had thought of the solution. Even if they don't have the final say about what is to be done, participation in devising alternatives or in considering the merits of each option will help your people feel they've helped in the decision making. That is, as long as you are honest about it and *really* consider their ideas.

Another reason to work in groups is that they often come up with better ideas than a person working alone might. More possible solutions will be generated, as each person has a different frame of reference. So the more diverse the group (in experience, education, etc.), the more possible points of view you'll get. This usually results in a much richer range of ideas.

And if the problem involves something your people will have to implement, you certainly want input from their vantage point. After all, they are familiar with the operation. You may focus on results and costs, but they will see the actual process and be more aware of bugs that might show up in the nuts and bolts.

Groups Require Leadership. A group without any leader at all usually disintegrates. In order to accomplish something, the leader must continually direct the group to its purpose. This requires control. At the same time, the atmosphere must be safe and permissive in order for people to participate freely.

To start with, let people know that you're interested in *every* idea, that no one will be penalized later for things said in a meeting, and that everyone's ideas will be treated with equal respect.

As the leader you also have a responsibility to make sure everyone gets an equal chance to participate. That means you'll have to tactfully shut up the guy who monopolizes the meeting by running off at the mouth. And you'll have to encourage the wallflowers to speak up: "OK, Charlie, let's hear what Gus has to say about that idea."

How to Turn the Group Off. If your subordinates feel that you have a personal interest in a particular point of view, they are likely to avoid criticizing it, even if they disagree. For this reason, make a special effort to encourage criticism and show that you are flexible. Having your mind made up before you ask them about something is manipulative and insulting. After you do this once or twice, you're not likely to get anything but yesses at the next discussion.

If you really *don't* want your subordinates' participation in a project, at least let them know where they stand: "This project is complete and I'm not looking for any new ideas on it. I just want you to look it over to see what we're doing." Don't ask for a subordinate's opinion unless you're really willing to listen and change. Don't fish for approval, either—you'll usually end up dissatisfied with what you get.

Notes on Assertive Supervision

1. Give your subordinates as much control over their own work and work environment as possible.
2. Let your employees know, in clear, straightforward language, exactly what you expect of them.
3. Never assume your subordinates *know* what you want. *Tell* them. Don't make them guess what you are after.
4. When a subordinate does something wrong, improper, or irritating, let him know about it right

away, in a tactful manner. Let him know that it bothers you. "Ursula, I'm upset with your spending so much time on personal phone calls."

5. Make sure you have a clear idea of what your goals are before asking your subordinates to carry them out.

6. Treat subordinates consistently; that is, don't play favorites, and try not to let fluctuations in your moods influence your behavior.

7. Give clear verbal instructions; *demonstrate whenever possible;* and ask questions to be sure a trainee has understood your message. Give a new person lots of support when he's starting out. Be available when he needs you, and follow up to be sure he has understood what you want.

8. Never belittle an employee for making a mistake or not knowing something. Treat the subordinate and his problems with respect.

9. Don't expect perfection. People grow by learning from their mistakes. Treat errors matter-of-factly. Concentrate on correcting them, not on pointing them out.

10. Don't forget positive feedback. Give your subordinates praise whenever it's sincere and justified. If you think they're doing a good job, let them know it. (They can't read your mind here, either.)

11. Give your subordinates room to grow. When they show the capability, give them more responsibility. As soon as they show they can handle it, back off and give them space to do the job the way they see fit.

12. Give subordinates as much background information as possible. Let them know *why* things need to be done, how their jobs fit into the overall picture.

13. If employees persist in undesirable behavior, persist in telling them about it. Confront them with the problem and try to get to the bottom of it, the real reason behind their insubordination.

14. When it becomes obvious that the employee won't change, even when confronted with the possibility of dismissal, fire him as quickly as possible.

15. Involve your subordinates in problem solving and

decision making whenever their input might be useful and wherever the decisions concern their work.

16. Don't ask for a subordinate's opinion unless you're really willing to listen and change.

section two

AN ASSERTIVE STAND WITH YOUR BOSS

How do you handle the relationship with your boss? Do you feel weak and powerless? Do you keep complaints to yourself rather than express them? Are you afraid to ask for things?

When you do make complaints and ask for things, how do you go about it? Do you hint and beat around the bush, hoping he'll get the message? Do you demand your way from a base of righteousness and logic? And how do you act when you don't get your way?

Once Again, It's a Matter of Attitude. An assertive person is self-confident. When he takes a job, he promises to give fair work for his wages. He knows that the boss will judge the worth of his work, and even assess some of his behavior.

But his ultimate worth as a human being is a very private matter. He doesn't sell his soul. He reserves the right to keep his own opinions and values.

Let's clarify the distinction between judging the human being and judging his behavior. Whatever you don't like about a person can be broken down into a series of his actions, or instances of behavior. Suppose, for example, Mel is a nosy type who always wants to know everyone's business. You can give Mel a label and write him off altogether, or you can take assertive action when he displays the behavior you don't like. We're not saying you'll end up loving him—or everyone else around you— but before you condemn a person as an untouchable, at least give him or her a chance to change by assertively requesting it.

In the same way, people may judge you and your

personality. Their judgment isn't the final word on your worth as a person. It is up to you to decide for yourself the good and bad of your actions, the behavior you want to continue and the behavior you want to stop.

However, every act of behavior has its consequences. If everyone around you hates what you do, you may end up with no friends, no job, etc. But you have the right to be your own final judge, to look at the likely consequences of your actions and decide what course of action—and set of consequences—you wish to choose.

The important thing is that *you* are making the choice. If you bow to a convention you don't believe in, do it to get the results you want.

In the work world, as in every area of life, our values will sometimes conflict with other people's. The rational person assesses the conflicts and their possible consequences. Then he chooses—whether to go along with certain things, or not to.

Any group of people sets the norms for what is acceptable behavior in that group. At some parties you can take off your clothes and be a hit. At others, you'd be ushered out the door. If you flaunt what the group considers to be undesirable behavior, you are asking to be expelled.

But excessive, unwarranted worry about losing your job is unassertive. If you are always worried that something you do or say might lead to dismissal, you'll be afraid to state your opinions and desires. It will cripple your ability to function freely.

The truth of the matter is that the person who is superworried about losing his job is more likely to lose it than someone who isn't. A person who feels free to speak his mind honestly is a much more valuable employee than someone who is afraid to say anything but "Yes." This is particularly so where the freedom comes from a healthy, objective appraisal of reality, including a proper sense of one's own worth, rather than from neurotic impulses, such as a self-defeating need to show up everybody else—including the boss.

Sometimes the result of being open and straightforward *will* lead to termination of your employment. But that often will be for the best. Many people have gone on to new and far better jobs and careers as the result of being fired.

In one case, a young woman was working as a bookkeeper for a small company. The company office manager/accountant taught her how to do a lot more than plain bookkeeping; when he left, she did his job. But when she said she wanted higher pay for doing a more complex and more important job, the boss fired her. This motivated her to return to school and get her master's in accounting so she could qualify for the title and money she thought she should be making. She's now a lot further along in her career than she would have been if she had stayed in that company meekly collecting her old salary.

Often It's How You Say It, Not What You Say, That Counts. As pointed out earlier, you can say almost anything as long as you do it properly. This means taking into consideration the other person's point of view: imagining how they feel about what you're saying. Talking straight—and taking responsibility for your message. Finally, it means speaking in a nonthreatening manner.

When something is bothering you, don't complain to your co-workers or mope about the office. If it's something you must see the boss about, don't rush into him in anger, either. Sit down and figure out exactly what is bothering you and why. Gather the facts about the situation—what you really know, versus mere rumor and mind-reading.

Then plan a simple, direct way to state your complaint to the boss. Relax. Take a few deep breaths. Try not to be angry. Be sure your voice won't crack with tears or bad feelings. Now go in and talk to him—or her.

Marge, a new employee in the personnel department, was reviewing employee benefits. She asked a co-worker whether an employee's Blue Cross-Blue Shield family coverage was paid for by the company. The co-worker said they paid for a man's family coverage, but not a woman's.

Marge saw red and was about to rage into her boss's office. But she did the right thing and checked her facts first. As it turned out, families of all "breadwinners"

119

were covered, whether they were men or women. Her co-worker had the wrong information.

Les, an editor at a small publishing company, was expecting a new assignment to be handed over to him. When he overheard his boss giving the assignment to someone else, Les felt as if he had been kicked. He started to think of all sorts of bad reasons why he hadn't gotten the assignment, all leading to the same message: The boss didn't think he was good enough to handle it.

But Les remembered his assertiveness training and decided to approach his boss:

> LES   Bob, I overheard you giving the Winter Day assignment to Jim, and I'm bothered because I had expected this assignment to be turned over to me.
>
> BOB   Oh, I'm glad you came in, Les. I'm working on a big package that's going to come through any day now. And that's the project I have in mind for you.
>
> LES   Oh, I'm relieved to hear that. I thought you might have had some doubt as to my ability to handle Winter Day.
>
> BOB   None at all, Les. But this other thing is going to take up too much of your time. It's the kind of assignment I think you'll enjoy more, too.
>
> LES   Great.
>
> BOB   But I'm glad you told me what was on your mind, Les. I appreciate your doing that.

Les stopped trying to read the boss's mind and *asked* him what was on it. Most bosses will appreciate it, just as Bob did.

Whenever you have vague feelings of disfavor, find out what the score is. Go directly to the source. If your boss *is* dissatisfied with your work, you should find out about it anyway so you can figure out what you did wrong and how to improve.

You might question the advisability of Les's admitting that he thought his boss had doubted his ability. As a regular practice, we recommend that you simply ask questions and wait for the answers rather than expressing your doubts. But if you know your boss well and feel he or she is the type you can level with, there's no harm in admitting anxiety once in awhile. Furthermore, Les didn't jump to a negative conclusion and act on it by storming into the boss or something equally inappropriate. Instead he calmly said that he was bothered and explained why.

Taking Criticism. Bosses appreciate subordinates who can take criticism without becoming hurt, defensive, or argumentative. The best way to handle it is matter-of-factly. Realizing that you're going to make mistakes no matter how careful and clever you are should help you to have a good, open attitude about it.

When a simple mistake is pointed out, admit it, accept it. Show that you understand why it was a mistake and that you will do your best to avoid it in the future: "Oh, you're right. I'll watch out for that next time."

But accept your mistake simply and briefly. There's no need for lengthy, groveling apologies. If it can be corrected, you'll correct it. If it can't—you're sorry for the error, and that's all.

Jeanne, a public accounting supervisor, saw a job fouled up because she didn't properly supervise Bill, her assistant. Jeanne's manager was upset because the job was essentially a simple one.

When Jeanne's manager told her how he felt about Bill's work, Jeanne said, "Well, he wasn't very well supervised." In other words, rather than becoming defensive and making up excuses, she admitted that she hadn't done a good job with Bill.

The result was that the manager laughed and brushed the matter off. He knew that Jeanne had been very busy with a lot of other things, so he was inclined to excuse her mistake rather than carry on at length about the poor job Bill had done.

When criticism goes beyond the indication of a simple mistake, the important thing is to learn from it— find out what you are doing wrong and how you can change or improve. The method here, just as in the chapter on handling criticism, is to ask for feedback:

PETE   Mr. G., I'd like to know why my bonus was so small this time.

MR. G   I'm afraid you haven't been pulling your weight, Pete.

PETE   What specifically is the problem?

MR. G   Costs in your department have gone up 15 percent, compared to the company average of 8 percent.

PETE   But the cost of raw materials has sky-rocketed, too.

MR. G   That might account for part of the increase, but not all of it. Your labor costs have been too high.

PETE   That's true—but we've been forced into an awful lot of overtime in order to meet production schedules.

MR. G   That may be, Pete, but overtime is a short-term solution, not a long-term one. Why didn't you talk to me before about this problem?

PETE   I don't know. I should have. Maybe we can work on it now.

MR. G   Good. Let's do that.

If the boss comes up with a legitimate gripe, the best thing to do is work out ways to improve the situation. If you need to, ask his advice. In fact, whenever you find yourself stumped, don't simply keep living with a bad situation. Ask for help. And when you do, make sure you know exactly what your problem is. Have the contributing factors clear in your mind. Write down the main points. Then list the solutions you've tried or considered and why they didn't or won't work. If you come up with any other possibilities, list them, too. Being prepared in this way will save your boss a lot of time and effort and make him think a whole lot more of you.

What if the Boss's Criticism Isn't Justified? One morning, Debbie, an audit supervisor, got a call from a partner asking for a particular memo, one that was not yet ready. She said, "This is April first. The memo has no effect until August. And I have priority items that are due in two weeks." She felt the memo wasn't a priority item, and in *her* overall work picture it wasn't. But *his* work schedule, naturally, was independent of hers—and he still wanted the letter when he wanted it.

Noting that she was upset, however, he asked her what was wrong. She pointed out all the other things she had to take care of and described the pressure she was under. But at the end she said, "I'll take care of it."

The partner was so impressed by her busy schedule that he called the other partners and complained that she had too heavy a workload at that time.

Debbie had said how she felt, and she had given reasons for the delay on the memo. But she went a step further: She had the letter ready for him the next day. We asked Debbie if she thought that was necessary since she already had adequately explained why it was late. She said, "No. But it made the partner even more appreciative because he realized that in spite of all the other work I had, I wanted to please him."

You don't have to accept unjustified criticism, as long as you handle it properly. The important thing is to show that you're trying to do a good job—that you, too, care about end results, just like the boss does. And phrase your rebuttal so that you leave your boss's pride intact: "I guess you didn't realize that . . ." "Perhaps you didn't notice it, but . . ."

If you cannot convince your boss that you're right, it's usually best to accept his opinion and let it drop. This is especially true if the matter is inconsequential. If it's something major that will affect the company in a substantial manner, you should insist—and, if necessary, take the matter higher. You don't want to be sitting there saying "I told you so" when the company faces a $50,000 loss. And if you do go higher, but no one listens, and there's a $50,000 loss, *don't* say, "I told you so."

Going Over the Boss's Head. If your boss is generally fair and square with you and fights for "his" people, you're probably better off taking all your ideas and complaints directly to him and letting *him* fight the higher-ups. You might suggest on occasion that you go along with him to supply backup details in a particular presentation. You can also supply him with written materials for this purpose.

If your boss is ineffectual, you'll probably have to learn to live with the situation, look for another job, or request a transfer. If you decide to stay where you are, keep quiet and do a fantastic job in your own area. If you complain about your boss to *his* boss, you may be the one who is let go.

On the other hand, your boss may be the kind of person who isn't concerned about reporting lines. He may be happy to have you contact his boss when appropriate.

Making Requests. When you want something, the best thing to do is to ask for it in a straight, direct, positive way:

"I'd like to take Friday off."

"I want to attend a seminar on marketing in February."

"I need a budget increase."

Back up your requests by telling the benefits to be gained or the other reasons. For example:

"I think the ideas exchanged at the seminar will help us a lot."

"We've had an unexpected increase in equipment costs."

And it helps greatly to make it easy for your boss to grant your request: John, a management consultant, was concerned about the kind of assignments his firm was giving him. First he thought, "If I go in and say that to the boss, what will his reaction be? What is he going to want from me?" Realizing that his boss was very busy, John thought it best to walk in with a definite plan in order to make maximum use of the time his boss could spare for their discussion.

So he outlined his current workload and laid out a

six-month schedule, indicating available time. He told his boss he felt he could handle certain types of assignments in the time frame, that he would like to do them, and that he wanted the boss to arrange to get him this type of work.

John's boss asked for a copy of the schedule. By that afternoon he had lined up a couple of the jobs John wanted.

If you just dump a problem in your boss's lap he might not have the time or inclination to think of a solution. But if you guide him in the direction you want to go—offering possible ways to proceed—you're much more likely to get what you want.

Use Positive, Firm Language. It's amazing how often people will start requests with negative wording, such as,

"I don't know if you can help me, but . . ."

"It may not be the right time to bring this up, but . . ."

"It's probably too much to ask, but . . ."

"You're probably not interested in this, but . . ."

Jim's boss always edited his reports. Whenever Jim disagreed with a change his boss had made, Jim would go to him and say something like, "Do you think this is clear?" or "Do you think this might be said a better way?" Sometimes his boss would agree with him, but it would take a lot of haggling and the boss was never very happy with his complaint.

After discussing the problem in an assertiveness training session, Jim tried something new. He said very positively, "This line isn't clear to me. I think it should be . . ." His boss quickly and cheerfully agreed to change it.

Jim's revised statement worked because it was simple and direct. He said exactly what he meant instead of asking vague questions. Previously, his boss had probably wondered what he was trying to get at. Also, Jim offered the boss a concrete alternative, making it simple for him to agree with Jim's change.

Asking for Money. People always ask us for assertive methods of asking for money and other benefits. Many of them feel that they are not being paid what they should be. Yet they hesitate to do anything about it. They take what they get—and complain to their spouse.

But as we keep saying, the way to get something is to *ask for it.* Anybody who ever has taken a sales training course has had this message drummed into his consciousness: *Ask for the order.*

Sandy felt that she wasn't being paid as much as other people doing her level of work. When it was time for the company's annual salary review, she went to her immediate boss and told him this. They discussed the matter and he said he'd think about it.

The next step in the review was an interview with the head of the department. Sandy kept talking around the issue, discussing everything but money, for about an hour. The department head kept saying, "Well, do you have anything else to talk about?"

Finally Sandy said, "There is the matter of salary." At that point he burst out laughing and said, "I thought you would take forever to say it!"

Sandy ended up getting the largest increase of anyone in her department. But she wouldn't have if she hadn't spoken up.

Timing is important. In Sandy's company there was an annual review time when everyone's work was evaluated and raises were given out. Sandy didn't ask for the raise at mid-year, because her company had an inflexible rule about the matter.

A good time to ask for a raise is at the point when you've just been recognized for some particularly valuable contribution to your company. Certainly the worst time would be after a colossal goof-up.

Also consider your boss's *personal* timing. Pick a day when he's in a good mood. Avoid times when he's under a lot of stress, especially where the pressure on him involves money worries.

When considering the appropriate time or the amount of money to ask for, don't be too concerned with "the way things have always been done." Sure, in certain organizations—such as Sandy's—there may be a real taboo. But it usually doesn't hurt to try. Just because *most* people are reviewed after the first six months doesn't mean, for example, that you shouldn't ask for a raise after two months. If you have good reasons—go ahead.

If no one has ever gotten more than a 15 percent increase, don't let that stop you from asking for 20 percent. If you work for a small, flexible organization this kind of thing is easier to swing. But even when there are rulebooks that say they can't do it, larger organizations may find a way to make an exception for the right person.

"The right person"—that's the key. If you are valuable to the company, and if they want to keep you, you have a lot of leverage. This doesn't apply only to those in upper echelons. Value is relative. A file clerk can be very valuable compared with others in that position. Somebody who is accurate, punctual, cooperative, and rarely sick is valuable to a company—and to a supervisor—and may be worth a raise even though it isn't review time.

As with any other request, be as specific as possible when asking for money. Have an amount in mind. Have reasons why you should get it. Sandy's reason was that people doing the same type of work she was doing were making a lot more money than she was. You may simply feel you are worth more to the company. If you can back this up with examples, such as increased sales, money saved, efficiency increases, etc., all the better.

If you don't have an amount in mind, you won't know how to respond when the boss makes you an offer. Of course, asking for something outrageous may irritate your boss. You should have an idea of what is reasonable—and ask for a bit more.

And when you ask, use a positive tone of voice, and an inflection to match. Don't let your voice rise at the end of a declarative sentence or it ends up: "I'd like a $2,000 raise???"

If you find it especially difficult to ask for a raise, simply getting yourself into the boss's office and bringing up the subject may be all you can expect from yourself the first time. You might start out by saying, "May I speak with you a moment?" When he asks, "About what?" say, "Money." If all else fails in your efforts to force yourself to raise the subject, just walk in and blurt out: "I'd like to talk about money."

One of the great things about forcing yourself to do this, no matter how difficult it might be the first time, is that you'll find yourself becoming more confident. Sandy said that once she discovered she got what she asked for, she started asking for more things. "Now I feel as though I'm more in control of the situation."

When Sandy left her company for a better job, she found that even being assertive at an exit interview can mean more money. She was asked to rate her company on compensation and she rated it very low. When asked why, she gave several reasons. Then she was interviewed by the head of the department, who had all sorts of statistics to "prove" that Sandy was wrong. But she stuck to her guns, and told him, too, why she felt the way she did.

Months later, when she went to get her bonus check for the year, she found that her bonus had been increased because of her comments at the exit interview.

Don't Look a Gift Horse in the Mouth. Just as important as asking for things is showing appreciation when you get something. If your boss gives you a raise or does you a favor, thank him for it. Even if you don't get *exactly* what you want, let him know you appreciate what you did get. He may have done the best he could, even if your increase was small.

If people stroke you and you don't stroke them back, they're going to stop trying to do something for you. If you never stop complaining, no matter what you get, they'll think: "We'll never make him happy, so why bother trying?"

Along this same line: Be careful about how much and how often you ask for things. Some assertiveness books advocate asking for things just for the sake of asking for them. We disagree. We don't suggest asking your boss for a new filing cabinet just to *prove* you are assertive. Asking for things *all* the time can become downright obnoxious.

If you find yourself constantly butting up against people, you don't need assertiveness, but a reevaluation of your motivation. Maybe you simply enjoy con-

128

flicts. Or maybe you are bent on some sort of self-destruction.

Assertiveness is a tool; like any other tool, it can be abused. Some people take any new method that comes along and use it to pursue their same old neurotic goals. They use it as an excuse for continuing to mess up their lives: "Listen, getting fired wasn't *my* fault. I was just practicing my assertiveness."

One of the basic premises of this book, in fact, is that you look at the world as realistically as possible and take responsibility for the consequences of your actions. If things continue to fall apart around you, check *yourself* out. If you can't do it alone, get professional help. It's important. It's your life.

You Won't Always Get What You Want. No matter how assertive you are, you won't always win or get what you want. Sometimes you may have to settle for less, sometimes for nothing. The important thing is that you tried. You should feel good about yourself because you did your best.

Don't be unduly concerned over what's *fair,* either. It may not be *fair* that another manager is earning $5,000 more than you, but if that's what he was able to negotiate for—good for him. If you can negotiate for an equivalent increase—more power to you, too. If you don't get it, there's no point in pining over the "unfairness" of it. Look around you; a lot of things in life are not meted out according to what's fair.

It's important to keep your perspective: negotiate hard in the negotiating room, but shake hands with your opponent afterwards. Once a decision is made, forget the argument. Live with the consequences of your negotiations, and don't hold grudges. Remember —you won't *always* be on the right side of a dispute!

Meetings. Go to meetings—especially planning meetings—prepared. If you have an idea or proposal you want the group to adopt, write it up carefully ahead of time and provide each participant with a copy. Your plan should show the results to be obtained, the steps to get there, costs, etc.

The group thus is more likely to take your plan and use it, or at least use it as a guideline to be modified. You may be put in charge of the program; at the least you'll get credit for having designed it. Whereas if you simply throw out ideas at a meeting, other people will take them, write them up, and get the credit. Also, people have difficulty visualizing the implementation and results of an idea. By working it up into something more substantial, you will give them a better picture of what you have in mind. And you'll show them that there's a practical way to accomplish it.

Presenting Ideas to Your Boss. People who make it a habit of throwing their ideas out to co-workers often are afraid of taking responsibility for their ideas. (It's true that they won't get into trouble if anything goes wrong—but they also won't get credit when the idea works.)

Your best bet is to write all your ideas down. Keeping a written list is necessary—*many excellent, important ideas are never tried because they've simply been forgotten.* When you have an idea whose time has come, that you consider workable, get the details you need from your staff, and then write up the idea as thoroughly as possible. Indicate what benefits can be expected, how the idea can be implemented, what it will cost, who might do it, etc. Then send a short report memo on it to your boss and other interested parties.

Depending on the nature of the idea, you may wish to hold a briefing after the reports have been distributed. Or you may simply wish to present the idea orally to your boss. If so, have the written back-up with you when you do. Hand him a copy to look at while you talk to him. When people have things in black and white, it helps them listen and understand, and it usually comes across as a stronger proposition.

Keep your eyes and ears open for ideas from other people—you know, those people who throw them into the air because they don't want to take responsibility for them or are too lazy to work them up into something solid. When they toss out their gems, make a mental note of the good ones and write them down as soon as you can. If you can turn such thoughts into practicalities, give the idea-generator due credit in your report. You'll get enough kudos for having spotted it as something useful.

Taking an Assertive Stand With Your Boss

1. You can say almost anything to your boss if you:
   a) Consider his point of view;
   b) Talk straight—take responsibility for your message: "I want . . ." "I am bothered by . . .";
   c) Speak in a nonthreatening, conversational tone;
   d) Have the background facts and presentation clear in your own mind first.

By now, you are well aware that the first three are your assertive way of dealing with just about everybody, not just your boss. And the fourth point isn't a bad general rule either.

2. Never jump to conclusions. Always check rumors thoroughly. Don't attempt to read your boss's mind.
3. Accept the blame for your mistakes. Let the boss know you're willing to correct them, and ask for his help if necessary.
4. If the boss criticizes you unjustly, let a little time pass, and then tactfully point out his mistake when the two of you are alone. But don't be picky on this issue; if the point is minor, let it pass. The important thing is to show the boss that you care about end results, just as he does.
5. When you want something, ask for it. Do so in a direct, positive way. Back up your requests with benefits and reasons and a plan all worked out to make it as simple as possible for your boss to grant it.
6. Avoid negative language, such as,

   "I don't know if you can help me, but . . ."
   "It's probably too much to ask, but . . ."

7. If you want to be paid more money—ask for it. Time your request to coincide with your boss's good mood, an appropriate review time, and your own outstanding performance. Be specific as to the amount you want. Have some reasons as to why you deserve a raise.

8. When you get something close to what you wanted, thank the person responsible for your getting it.

9. Bargain hard in the negotiating room, but accept the results amiably. Don't hold grudges.

10. Protect your ideas by writing them down. Work them up as fully as possible. See that important people get copies of your proposals.

11. Remember that the worst possible consequence of speaking up might be losing the job—and that is *not* the end of the world. (In fact, it frequently is the beginning of a better one.)

section three

WOMEN IN MANAGEMENT

Women should understand men—and themselves— better. Men should understand women—and themselves—better. The other chapters of this book deal with problems of people-to-people relationships at work. This chapter deals with the same problems, particularly in those situations where male-female factors are involved.

Although the thrust of the first part of this section is toward women and the second toward men, both will benefit from the entire section. Both men and women are finding themselves exposed to male-female relationships that were uncommon in the past. Men used to dealing with women strictly as low-level subordinates now may find them as peers and even superiors. Women used to dealing with other women strictly as peers now may be supervising them, or reporting to them. As women move up in management, they will become some men's peers, and finally their superiors.

Because of the enormous stirrings of change in our times, there is confusion over roles, particularly woman's. *Is* there a role? If so, what is it? Should a "management woman" behave in a certain way because she is a woman? And so on. Men who have spent all their lives taking care of women, telling women what to do, expecting women to be in the weaker, more emotional, more subordinate role, may have a difficult time adjusting to the changes. And women have to cope with the other side of those changes. Neither sex realizes that it is not the only one with these problems —both are being confronted with complex readjustments.

A man forms his idea of women from his mother, his sisters, his wife, his daughters—and from society's attitudes toward all of them. No matter what statistical proofs there are, or how independent, forceful, and capable are the women he sees on the job, he will tend to keep the old image.

Our judgments are greatly colored by how we perceive our experience. If all the women we know have difficulty with math, we're likely to think that's a trait of women—even if a female mathematical whiz turns up at the office.

It's not going to be easy to change attitudes, opinions, and deep-seated beliefs. In fact, it's not advisable to try to do so directly. As we pointed out earlier, opinions are formed not only by logic and reasoning, but by the emotional factor as well. This includes all the experience we've lived through, all the attitudes we've been brought up with.

Let's face it—both men and women have cause to fear the new roles based on equality of the sexes. Anything new is frightening to some degree. Having a clearly defined role to play at least offered some security, some direction to one's life. People who have been approaching life in a particular way, and then are told that that way is no longer valid, will be anxious, fearful, distrustful. They will feel threatened; without realizing it, they will be unsure of their own adequacy to meet the new challenges. This is the worst fear of all. And if we fear the reality that facts and logic show us, we will look for a way to discredit those facts.

To Women

The point of this discussion is to help women see the male point of view sympathetically—i.e., with understanding and empathy. It is also to caution you not to expect quick changes in attitudes and beliefs.

Are we saying there's nothing you can do? *No! There*

is plenty you can do! The point is to put your efforts into changing *behavior,* not attitudes. It's a lot easier to get a man to stop *calling* you "honey" than it is to get him to stop *thinking* of you as "honey."

If you want a man to stop calling you "honey," having an argument with him on equality of the sexes is not the way to go about it. Forget about changing his opinions and beliefs. Instead, work on getting him to change his behavior. Use the same assertive communication skills that we've discussed in earlier chapters.

It's amazing how consistently people overlook the simplest method of all: ASK SOMEONE TO DO WHAT YOU WANT THEM TO DO.

Remember the model of assertive speech: I want you to . . .

"Jerry, I want you to stop calling me 'honey.' "

Use a calm, friendly, but firm tone of voice. Don't be sarcastic. Don't say it in anger.

If you run into problems, continue to use assertive verbal techniques:

> JERRY Oh, Sue, I just do it without thinking because I like you.
>
> SUE I understand, Jerry, and I'm glad you like me, but I'd like you to stop doing it from now on anyway.
> [Sue is being persistent, but showing empathy for Jerry's feelings.]
>
> JERRY I hope you're not becoming one of those women's libbers?
>
> SUE I may be.
> [She is deflecting his criticism. If she wants to find out more about what Jerry thinks about women's libbers, she might prompt Jerry to reveal his feelings:]
>
> SUE What is it about being a liberated woman that's bad?
>
> JERRY They hate men.

134

SUE   You're worried that I'll begin to hate
        you if I become a liberated woman?
JERRY   Yeah.
        [Note that Sue is not trying to read
        Jerry's mind by assuming what he
        means. She gives him a chance to ex-
        press his thoughts and concerns.]

SUE   Well, I can see why it bothers you,
        then. But I've always liked men well
        enough and I probably will continue
        to do so.
JERRY   Then what's so bad about me calling
        you "honey"?
SUE   I just don't like it, Jerry.
JERRY   I wouldn't mind if you called *me*
        "honey."
SUE   I understand, but I don't like it.
JERRY   O.K., I'll try to stop doing it.
SUE   Thanks.

Note that Sue doesn't have to have a good *explanation* of why she wants Jerry not to call her "honey."
The fact that she doesn't like it is reason enough. We
don't have to justify, or rationalize, or explain our likes
and dislikes to anyone.

Let People Know What You Want. And let them
know what's bothering you. For example, if there's a
meeting you weren't invited to and you think you
should have been, don't jump to the conclusion that
"they" are deliberately picking on you. Don't sulk and
complain about it to your co-workers—and certainly
don't mention it to your subordinates. As soon as you
find out about it, go *immediately* to the person responsible for the meeting and tell him what's bothering you:

JANICE Fred, you just called a meeting that I
        feel I should have been invited to.
        [She simply states the facts of what
        happened and how she feels. She
        doesn't assume Fred had a particular
        motivation.]
FRED   Oh? Gee, I'm sorry Janice. I didn't
        even think of you!

135

JANICE   I'll accept your apology, Fred, if you'll
         fill me in on what happened, and be
         sure to invite me to the next one.

FRED   Sure.

If Fred invites Janice to the next meeting, her problem is solved. In many cases, this is what will happen
if we are direct and assertive in our demands without
aggressively accusing the other person of slighting or
discriminating against us.

But suppose Fred later holds another meeting without inviting Janice?

JANICE   Fred, I'm really bothered that you
         didn't ask me to the meeting again.

FRED   But Janice, it was just an informal get-
         together. You weren't around, that's
         all. I didn't *plan* not to ask you. Be-
         sides, Ralph can fill you in on what
         we talked about.

JANICE   Fred, I'd like you to call me for the
         next meeting. I don't like to be left
         out, no matter what the reason.

FRED   O.K., Janice, I'll try.

Janice can continue to bug Fred until he starts inviting her to meetings. Or if Janice can get the cooperation of other members of her group, she can ask them
to let her know when there is a meeting. Then she can
simply show up at it. This will eliminate Fred's excuse
that he "didn't think of her," or that she "wasn't
around at the time."

Suppose you're in a situation where you're pretty
sure the boss hasn't asked you to a meeting because
you're a woman. Yet he makes up other excuses:

CYNTHIA Mr. K., I feel I should have been at
         the meeting you just had with Ted,
         Ronny, and Stan.

MR. K.   Cynthia, I didn't leave you out be-
         cause you're a woman. The topic of
         the meeting didn't concern you. We

	discussed the promotional budget for GLEARO.
CYNTHIA	But I work on the promotions for GLEARO.
MR. K.	Sure—the creative end. But you shouldn't worry your head about the numbers. We'll take care of that.
CYNTHIA	But I'm interested in the numbers, Mr. K. I'd like to sit in on these meetings in the future.
MR. K.	But it would be a waste of your time.
CYNTHIA	I don't feel that way, Mr. K. The more I know about things, the better the job I'll be able to do. And since I'm working on the ads, I may have something useful to contribute. I wish you'd give me a try.
MR. K.	All right, Cynthia, I will.

Keep stressing how important it is for you to know what's going on, how anxious you are to learn more about the larger picture; and if you have anything solid you may be able to contribute, point this out. But never accuse him of being unfair, of picking on you because you're a woman. If he says, "I'm not doing this because you're a woman," respond, "Oh, I know that, George, that's why I'm talking to you about it. I know you'll be fair."

It's most important to remain calm, to use a conversational tone of voice. Don't try to face the person when you're emotionally upset. Try to relax. Take a few deep breaths. Plan carefully what you will say, what he might say, how you will handle it.

Handling Male Clients. A woman CPA and senior auditor for a public accounting firm related this story about her experience:

"One of the more serious problems I had with a client was at a company where I had come in as the new senior accountant. The first day on the job their chief accountant told me he didn't like the fact that I was a woman.

"When I asked him what he meant, he said he had had very good rapport with the last auditor and felt he wouldn't have that same rapport with me. It was O.K. for women to work *for* you, but he didn't like to have to work on an equal level with one.

"My reaction to this was: 'Well, at least this guy is being frank with me and telling me honestly how he feels.' I told him I was sorry he felt that way, but since neither of us had any choice in the matter, I hoped as the job went on that he'd realize we could get along and get the job done. Then we made a few jokes and that was about it.

"The work I was doing at this place involved my asking a lot of questions and sending out various questionnaires to check out their systems. This accountant obviously didn't like my asking questions and was very ornery about it. He even lied to me in two instances. I tried to take it in stride, thinking he was just that kind of guy, and continued to do my work and ask my questions.

"A few days later I was called into the president's office for a talk. He and the treasurer said they had some 'fatherly advice' to give me. They said I had been coming off as very suspicious, and for my own good they wanted to warn me about it. But when I asked for specific details about who had said this and why, they refused to tell me.

"Since they were the client and I didn't want to blow the whole thing out of proportion, I kept my outrage to myself. I guess I didn't trust my instinctive reactions in this case and I didn't want to come across as an overly defensive woman. So I told them I was glad they had told me about it and that I would try to avoid this problem in the future.

"When I got back to my own office, I talked to some people there, including one of the partners, to see how they thought the situation should be handled. The partner said to cool it—that they were behind me and everything would work out all right. In fact, two months later the chief accountant who had complained about my being 'suspicious' was fired.

"The thing that bothered me most about this incident was that I don't think a man would have been treated in the same way. Even if a male auditor had in fact acted in a suspicious manner or done something wrong, he wouldn't have gotten that kind of 'fatherly' treatment.

"This incident happened about two years ago. If the same kind of thing happened to me today, I think I'd handle it differently. Instead of compliantly accepting guilt, I would be more assertive. After all, the firm's accountant was lying to the auditors. That wasn't doing his company any favors.

"It's not easy to know the appropriate behavior in every situation when you're treading in the delicate area of client relationships. In a professional field, such as public accounting, you have to be able to get along with people, in addition to having the technical skills.

"I've had several people on the job tell me that they like me, that I'm a very sharp, together person. They can see that I obviously enjoy what I'm doing and they approve of me. 'But yet,' they say, 'you're missing out on something and giving up some kind of femininity by being the way you are. You're a little bit too tough.'

"The problem is, what they call 'femininity' is that old stereotype of the compliant person who smiles all the time and gives in to everyone around her. If I were like that, I wouldn't be able to do the job I do and come off as an effective person. They see that what I am doing is working, and they like it, but because it's different from the way they're used to seeing women act, they can't understand it."

Yes, men may tell you you're not being "feminine" when you act assertive. But that's a criticism easily deflected:

> HARRY   By pushing so hard for what you want, you're losing your femininity, Ethel.
>
> ETHEL   That's true. I probably am losing what you call "femininity."
>
> HARRY   Doesn't that bother you?
>
> ETHEL   No.

In this case, Ethel doesn't care what Harry thinks. If she is interested in finding out what's behind his complaint, or getting him to think a little deeper about femininity, she might say, after Harry's comment about Ethel pushing hard:

139

ETHEL	What is it about trying hard to get what I want that's not feminine?
HARRY	Feminine women don't act like that because they know it puts men off.
ETHEL	Is it that you think women shouldn't want things?
HARRY	No, but they should try to get them in different ways. Men like to give women things, not feel forced to. Women should be more patient and wait for things to happen.
ETHEL	Why shouldn't they ask for what they want?
HARRY	Because it's tough for a man to say "no" to a woman.
ETHEL	You find it difficult to say "no" to a woman?
HARRY	Yeah. I don't feel I can treat a woman as rough as I can treat another guy.
ETHEL	May I suggest assertiveness training? I think it could help a lot.

This brings up a good point. Many men feel that they can't use the same language or be as tough on women as they are on men. So they avoid women. They don't invite them to meetings. They don't criticize them the way they would a male.

This makes it very difficult for a woman to get adequate feedback about her work, to be accepted in the male "group," etc. It's going to take work—to prove that you *can* be criticized and take the lumps as well as the men can.

You'll have to prove yourself, and use assertive techniques to get the men to talk to you, to face you with important issues, to give you responsibility, and to include you in their decision making.

Some women try to use being female to advantage. They think that if they cry or act emotional, the boss will be putty in their hands. But this is a manipulative technique that, even if it works, may backfire in the end. Would *you* want to have someone around who could manipulate you with tears?

You don't have to use "feminine wiles" to get what

you want. Nor do you have to become "manly." By being straightforward and honest with people, you'll eventually get the reputation of being a straight talker. People will learn that they can't manipulate you, and that they can criticize you without an emotional upset following. They can work out a compromise with you fairly and openly. They can expect you to speak your mind, express your wants and feelings.

It will take time. *But always keep in mind that you're trying to change behavior, not attitudes*. The attitudes usually follow much later, after a lot of accumulated experience. Some men's attitudes may never change. But that's their business. They have a right to their own beliefs—and their prejudices—just as you have a right to yours. The most you can demand is acceptable *behavior* toward you.

To Men

More and more women are demanding a crack at jobs previously held by men. No matter what your personal feelings are about this, the fact is that change is here. You can expect to see more women in management positions as time goes by.

Let's face it—since anything new is frightening to some degree, both men and women have cause to fear the new roles based on equality of the sexes. Having a clearly defined role at least offered some security, some direction to one's life. People who have been approaching life in a particular way and are then told that that way is no longer valid will be anxious, fearful, distrustful. They will feel threatened; without realizing it, they will be unsure of their own adequacy to meet the new challenges.

And these challenges are hitting both men and women right in the eye. Equal opportunity must be granted—that's a legal fact. But no matter what the legal facts are, no one can legislate personal relations. People have to work them out on their own. It's to your advantage to learn how to work with women as peers, as superiors, and as subordinates.

Basically, one uses the same good communication skills discussed throughout this book. Level with

141

women, tell them what you want, let them know if their behavior irritates you, etc.

You may find it difficult to treat women this way. If you've been brought up to "respect" women, to think of them as being offended by loud and harsh words, as needing protection, you may find it difficult to start treating them as "people." This may be especially troublesome if the women you deal with use any supposedly "feminine" tactics, such as crying.

As a preliminary step, try to become aware of your feelings and behavior around the women you work with. Do you tend to grant favors to women subordinates more than men, or vice versa? Are you hesitant to criticize a woman's work? Or her behavior?

How would you feel about a woman boss? Do you have one now? Would you take a position in which you would have a woman boss? What problems would you expect because of a woman boss? In what ways might you treat her differently than you would a man?

The next time you relate to a woman at work, be self-aware. Observe your behavior. Note any feelings of anxiety, of trying to please, of uneasiness or embarrassment.

We suggest this introspection because everyone is different. Some men have few problems working with any women. Others have no difficulty as long as the women are either peers or superiors. The difficulties vary from person to person. By discovering your personal problem spots, you can do something about them.

Here are some examples of how assertive straight-talking can help solve typical male-female work conflicts:

Jack has a new boss, a woman. When she holds a meeting, she often asks Jack and the other managers questions that are difficult to answer on the spur of the moment. This has been embarrassing and frustrating to Jack. After giving it some thought, he approaches his boss, Lena:

JACK	Lena, I've got a problem I'd like to talk to you about.
LENA	What's that, Jack?
JACK	At the meeting yesterday when you

	asked me such detailed questions, I simply didn't have the answers at my fingertips. I felt embarrassed in front of the other managers.
LENA	Oh, I'm sorry, Jack, but how was I to know you wouldn't have the answers? The only way I can find things out is by asking questions.
JACK	I realize that, Lena, so I thought we might find some other way to handle it.
LENA	How?
JACK	If you would give me a list of the questions ahead of time, I could get the information and bring it to the meeting.
LENA	That might work for some things, but a lot of questions come up in the course of the meeting. It's impossible for me to know ahead of time everything I might need to ask.
JACK	Hmmmm. How about if we recess the meeting for an information-gathering break?
LENA	That's not a bad idea. I've noticed you're not the only one having trouble with my questions. This would give everybody a chance to get the facts and present them later.
JACK	You could announce at the beginning of the meeting that you don't expect everyone to have information at their fingertips.
LENA	Yes. But perhaps it ought to be more than a recess. I think we should have a short introductory meeting, where we lay out the problems, and then give everyone a few days to do some fact-finding and exploratory work.
JACK	That sounds better yet. The final meeting should be a lot more productive.
LENA	Thanks for the suggestion, Jack.

Notice that Jack's approach was not scattershot: He talked about a specific instance of the behavior—yesterday's meeting—rather than saying "You always . . ." He didn't attack Lena, or say that what she did was wrong. Instead, he spoke about his own resultant feelings. And when he did, he spoke only of his own problem, not saying something like "All the guys think you're asking too many picky questions."

When his first suggestion didn't work, Jack tried to think of something else that would. He worked with Lena on a creative compromise; they solved their problem with mutual effort and respect.

JoAnn and Bob are co-workers. In addition to their management duties, from time to time they are required to compile special research reports for their boss. In the past, Bob and Jim, the man who had the job before JoAnn, always cooperated well on this. When one was especially busy, the other would take on any reports that had to be done. Bob expected the same cooperation from JoAnn but has not gotten it.

At first, to be considerate, Bob offered to do the reports because JoAnn was learning a new job. This continued for some months—and she still didn't offer to do her share.

Bob finally was so frustrated that when the boss assigned a big research project, Bob stormed into JoAnn's office and dumped it on her desk, saying it was about time she pulled her weight around the place. JoAnn started to cry. Bob mumbled apologies and left, taking the report with him.

What was wrong with the way Bob handled the incident? First of all, he waited so long to do something about a bothersome situation that his frustration built up to the boiling point. Secondly, he approached JoAnn aggressively, shouting and acting as if she had deliberately "wronged" him.

Let's look at a replay:

BOB	JoAnn, can I talk to you a minute?
JOANN	Sure, Bob, have a seat.
BOB	JoAnn, I'd like you to do this new research report the boss wants.

144

JoAnn	Gee, Bob, couldn't you do it? I have so much work piled up. I don't know where I'd find the time . . .
Bob	I understand your problem, JoAnn, but I feel I've done your share of the reports for you long enough. It's interfering with my own work. I want you to do this one.
JoAnn	Gee, I hate to confess this, Bob . . . but I have no idea how to go about doing those reports. I'm afraid I'll make a mess of it. [Starts to sniffle.]
Bob	[Ignoring sniffling] I'll be glad to show you how they're done. I'll leave this here so you can look it over. When you're ready to work on it, bring it over to my office and we'll talk about how you should start.

Bob spoke calmly and steadily throughout this encounter. He ignored JoAnn's emotional reaction because he knew he might not remain firm if he didn't. He offered to help, left the report, and walked out of her office, giving JoAnn a chance to pull herself together and adjust to the news that she would have to start doing the reports.

If Bob had felt confident, he might have expressed some empathy for JoAnn's feelings, such as, "I'm sorry you're upset over this, but I'll be glad to show you how to do the reports."

If JoAnn continued to give Bob a hard time by asking him to spend a lot of time helping her on every report she did, he'd have to be assertive once again:

Bob	JoAnn, I want you to do this next report on your own.
JoAnn	Oh, I'll never be able to do it on my own. I'll die without your help, Bob.
Bob	You may feel that way, JoAnn, but I still want you to try it.
JoAnn	Can I just ask you a few questions?

145

BOB	No. If you want me to review it when you're finished, I will. But that's all.
JoAnn	Have I done something wrong? Are you mad at me?
BOB	Nope. I just want to stop spending so much time on your reports.

Bob might have offered a compromise, such as giving JoAnn fifteen minutes to discuss questions about procedure on the report. On the other hand, if he felt she was simply using him and really didn't need his help, he might not even have offered to review the report for her.

The important thing is to act promptly, as soon as something starts to bother you. It's easier to take appropriate action then, instead of letting frustration and anger build up.

Ken has a new female assistant. As time goes by, he finds it harder and harder to get her cooperation. She doesn't fill him in on the work she's doing; she does what she considers high-priority items before the work he tells her to put first; and she seems to have more loyalty to other department heads than to him. He decides to face her with the problem:

KEN	Judy, I think it's time we straightened some things out between us.
JUDY	Oh?
KEN	I feel that you're resisting me, somehow.
JUDY	You mean I have a mind of my own?
KEN	No. Specifically, these are some of the things that are bugging me: I'd like you to touch base with me more often about what you're doing . . .
JUDY	You want an accounting of how I spend every minute?
KEN	Judy, is something bothering you??
JUDY	Since you brought it up, yes, there is something bothering me. You treat me as if I were an idiot, not your assistant

146

	—watching over every little thing I do—not giving me any real responsibility—you wouldn't dare treat a man like that!
KEN	Wow, you're really angry. (Nondirective listening.)
JUDY	I sure am!
KEN	I'd be angry, too, if I thought that was happening to me. (Empathy.)
JUDY	What do you mean, *thought*? You *have* been doing it!
KEN	I guess I have, from your point of view.
JUDY	What's *your* point of view?
KEN	I was worried about having a woman assistant, Judy. That's why I watched over you so carefully. I wanted to make sure everything went smoothly. Then, as soon as I saw you could handle it, I was going to ease up.
JUDY	Well, how do you think I felt being treated like that?
KEN	Lousy.
JUDY	Right. And, I admit, I wasn't too co-operative from that point on.
KEN	Out of frustration.
JUDY	Yeah. And then you became even more distrustful.
KEN	What a vicious circle we've been in!
JUDY	I should have spoken up right away and told you how I felt.
KEN	I should have, too. I'm awfully sorry about the bad start we got. Would you like to try again?
JUDY	I sure would.

Bob's complaints were symptoms of a deeper problem in his relationship with Judy. Because of her hostility, Judy was doing everything she could to sabotage Bob. This was self-destructive behavior for Judy, since it only aggravated her problem with Bob. If she had

147

spoken up about her feelings initially, the whole thing might have been avoided.

We have seen relationships break down totally because of this kind of situation. In one instance, the subordinate ended up with a stomach disorder because of the tension and eventually lost her job. Who knows what might have been accomplished if the two people had *really talked* to each other about what was bothering them?

To Women—A Summary

1. Work on changing men's offensive *behavior,* not their attitudes and beliefs.
2. Tell men what you want. Tell them what's bothering you:
   I WANT YOU TO . . .
   I AM BOTHERED BECAUSE . . .
3. Deflect criticism by agreeing with the truth in it. If you care what the person thinks, probe for feedback. Reassure him that you are not a man-hater.
4. Don't impugn motives or try to read minds. Assume the best intentions and act accordingly, until it's proven otherwise.
5. Don't let bad feelings build up. Speak up promptly to the person directly responsible for the situation bothering you.
6. Don't complain about a superior to co-workers and subordinates. Take your complaints to the source.
7. Be persistent. Don't give up the first time you don't get what you ask for.
8. Back up your requests with good reasoning. Go in with a plan.
9. Don't get emotional. Wait until you've calmed down. Take a few deep breaths. Talk in a calm, conversational manner.
10. Don't expect preferential treatment because you're a woman. Learn to take your lumps. The men do —and you can, too.
11. Try to learn from criticism. Own up to your mis-

takes simply and quickly, without exaggerated apologies. Remember that it's your behavior, not *you*, that's being criticized.

12. Relax. You don't have to be perfect. No one is.

To Men—A Summary

1. The women you work with may not want to be treated in the same manner you treat your wife, mother, daughters, etc. Look at your own behavior to see where it might be creating problems with the women you work with.

2. Don't try to read a woman's mind. *Ask* her. Get the facts. Speak up when something is bothering you.

3. Level with the women you work with. Use straight talking:
   I WANT YOU TO . . .
   I AM UPSET WHEN YOU . . .

4. Work on one specific problem at a time. Talk about actual recent behavior, not something old you've kept in all this time. And don't waste emotional energy talking about things that can't be changed.

5. Expect as much from women as you do from men. Give them the same responsibilities and challenges. Criticize them when it is appropriate. Forget the kid-glove handling.

6. If you feel there is trouble between you and a woman—whether subordinate, co-worker, or superior—try to get to the bottom of it. To get the woman to level with you, be a nondirective listener, and show empathy. Express your own feelings and needs. Try to work out a compromise. This will end up benefiting your department and your company, making your own performance look better than ever.

7. Don't be manipulated by tears. If you can't maintain calm composure in such circumstances, defer the meeting until the woman has regained control of herself:
   "I find it difficult to talk to you when you're upset

149

like this, so I'll leave now. Give me a call when you're feeling better and we'll continue."
8. Give women a chance. You'll be glad you did.

To Men and Women

Learn to laugh at yourselves. When a woman and a man hesitate in front of a door because he doesn't want to offend her by opening it for her, and she doesn't want to offend *him* by opening it for herself—that's a funny situation. If you can learn to laugh together, you can learn to work together.

EPILOGUE

We hope you enjoyed reading *Taking Charge on the Job*. As you were reading through the book you may have recognized yourself in some of the illustrations. That's good: Becoming aware of your responses to various situations is the first step on the road to change. Now it's up to you to decide what you want to accomplish and how you will go about doing it. Here are three suggestions to help you do this:

1. Reread the book. Now that you are familiar with the overall concepts, you can highlight and reinforce whatever was most appropriate to your needs, based on personality and job requirements.
2. If you want to follow up on assertiveness training either with additional readings or by experiencing the benefits of a workshop, information on both is given in the appendix.
3. Whenever you want a quick refresher on the points covered in the book, review the highlights summary on the next few pages.

The practices in this book work. They have worked for many others; they can work for you. Try them. Keep at it. If possible, work with a friend or co-worker. In the communications area, it helps to have an unbiased third party to hash things out with. It also helps to have their support when you're trying to change ingrained habits.

Above all, remember that *you* are responsible for your life, and you *can* make it better.

151

Summary of Main Points

1 Develop a Positive Self-Image

You are an important person with much to offer. Let the world know how good *you* are, and how good your *subordinates* are. When someone compliments you, accept it graciously—*you have earned it.*

2 Listen Effectively

• Focus on the actual words, gestures, and tone of the speaker.

• Abandon preconceived notions of what the speaker will say or what point of view he might have. Keep your mind open.

• Address your answer to what the person has *actually* said, not to what you think he might mean. If you feel the words don't reflect what was meant, ask the person to explain further.

• Don't jump to conclusions about people. Keep revising your picture of people as you get new information.

• Expect the best from people.

• To understand people when they talk to you, put yourself in their shoes. Try to imagine how they are thinking and feeling.

• When someone is upset about something, or has a problem, try to help them with nondirective listening: Repeat back to them, in your own words, what they have just said, emphasizing their *feelings* about the problem: "You feel you're getting a raw deal . . ." Don't argue, defend yourself, point out how they're being illogical, or try to give them solutions to their problem. Do as little talking yourself as possible. Give them plenty of room to open up.

- Don't read people's minds. Let them finish their own sentences.
- Don't spend listening time thinking of what you're going to say next. *Listen.*
- Don't expect other people to read *your* mind. *Tell* them what you want.

3 Make Sure People Hear You

- Make sure you have your listener's attention before you begin, and try to reach him when he's in a receptive frame of mind.
- Point out any possible benefits of your message. Give the listener a reason to *want* to hear you.
- Suit your language to your listener. Don't use terms that are too technical, sentences that are too complex, or ideas that are too abstract. Be concrete and specific whenever possible. On the other hand, don't oversimplify or talk down to people—they'll resent it, and you, and they'll stop listening.
- Be aware of emotional blocks to listening. If people are under stress, or suspect your motives, they won't hear you clearly.
- Try to start from a base of mutual understanding or agreement. Keep tuned in to your listener's point of view.
- Don't expect to win people over simply because you have logic on your side. You might win an argument with it, but logic won't necessarily change a person's feelings.
- Don't use policy and rules as a crutch. Explain the *why* of a rule. Don't be afraid to bend the rules when it makes sense to do so.
- Respect people's feelings, no matter how irrational they seem.
- Don't assume people have the same frame of reference and background you do. Fill them in. Tell them *more* than they need to know, if necessary, but not *less.*
- Don't assume people have understood you. Ask for feedback to make sure your message got through.

- Watch out when your mind switches to a new subject. Let your listener know you're on a new track.
- Be careful that people don't misread your humor. If you like to kid people sarcastically, you may be hurting someone who's especially sensitive and takes it the wrong way.
- Don't use humor when it's not appropriate. People may not like it if you first kid them about undesirable behavior and then seriously criticize them for it.
- Avoid becoming wedded to an opinion merely because you've said it or written it. Don't be afraid to say, "I changed my mind."
- Keep communication lines open. Don't be afraid to let the people under you know that you laugh and cry and bleed just like they do.

4 Take Responsibility for Your Messages

- Talk straight, putting the "I" where it belongs:
  "I want . . ."
  "I need . . ."
  "I don't like . . ."
- Tell people exactly what you want. Don't beat around the bush: "I want a raise." Not "It's tough living on my salary."
- If you want someone to do something, tell that person: "I want you to deliver this package," not "Someone's got to get this package delivered."
- Don't expect people to read your mind, take your hints, or share your values.
- Make your nonverbal messages match your verbal ones. For example, don't smile when you're trying to express anger.

5 Use Persistence to Get What You Want

- Speak in a calm, conversational, but firm voice. No matter what the other person says, don't become excited or angry.
- Keep repeating the message.
- Don't let yourself be sidetracked by excuses, accusations, other issues, etc.

- Get a commitment. If the person says "maybe" or "soon," try to pin him down to a specific time.
- Follow up to make sure the person is doing what you asked him to. Come back as many times as necessary until it's done.

6 Work Out a Compromise

- First, state your wants clearly.
- Persist in your original demand until you feel you are past the other person's excuses or manipulative counterargument.
- When you feel you've hit the bottom line, suggest a workable compromise or accept the other person's compromise.
- If your self-respect is in question, or if for any other reason you feel you can't accept the compromise, don't. Offer what you *can* accept, but be willing to take the consequences of no agreement.
- If you can't think on your feet, go back after you've had a chance to think things through, and re-negotiate. You may want to say, right in the initial negotiation, "I need time to think. I'll get back to you later."
- You don't have to make the "best deal" or a "fair deal." Make a deal you can live with.

7 Deflect Manipulative Criticism

- Agree with the truth or generalities in the critic's statement: "It's true, my hair is a different color today."
- Respond only to the actual *words* the critic says, not what is implied.
- Remember that no one can make you feel inferior unless you let them.
- Respond in a calm, conversational, matter-of-fact way.
- Do not defend yourself or attack the other person.
- If you have made a mistake, accept the mistake, but don't respond with guilt. If you want to apologize, keep it a simple, "I'm sorry."

• Probe vague criticism to find out specifically what you've been doing wrong: "What is it about my work that's second-rate, sir?"

• Keep probing until the other person comes up with the real reasons for the criticism.

• If he's not able to express it, prompt him with possibilities.

• No matter what is said, don't get defensive or act hurt. Think of the criticism as useful information that can help you do a better job in the future.

• Ask how you can change to improve, meet their requirements, etc., in the future.

• Especially when trying to get feedback from a passive, timid person, remember to remain sympathetic and keep any sarcasm or accusations out of your messages.

9 How to Handle Complaints or Criticism From Customers and Clients

• Listen to their problem, asking questions as necessary to find out exactly what's bugging them.

• Sympathize with their angry or upset feelings: "I'd be mad, too, if I were you."

• Show that you understand their problem.

• If you or your organization have made a mistake, admit it readily.

• *After* they've had a chance to express their feelings completely, offer to do the best thing possible to solve their problem.

• If you can't help them, or not in the manner they desire, let them know you're sorry about it. If possible, explain why you can't help them.

• Take whatever steps are necessary so that the problem is not likely to occur again.

10 Assertive Supervision

• Give your subordinates as much control over their own work and work environment as possible.

- Let your employees know exactly what you expect of them in clear, straightforward language.
- Don't ever assume people know what you want. *Tell* them; don't make them second-guess you.
- When a subordinate does something wrong, improper, or irritating, let him or her know about it right away, in a tactful manner. Let the other person know that it bothers you.
- Make sure *you* know what your goals are before you expect your subordinates to carry them out.
- Treat subordinates with consistency and impartiality. Try not to let fluctuations in your moods influence your behavior.
- Give clear verbal instructions. Demonstrate, when possible, and ask questions to be sure a trainee has understood your message. Give a new person lots of support when he's starting out. Be available when he needs you, and follow up to be sure he has understood what you want.
- Never belittle an employee for making a mistake or not knowing something. Treat the subordinate and his problems with respect.
- Don't expect perfection. People learn and grow through mistakes. Treat errors matter-of-factly and concentrate on correcting them.
- Don't forget positive feedback. If you think your subordinates are doing a good job, let them know it. They can't read your mind here, either.
- People need room to grow; give it to them. As they grow, give them more responsibility. As soon as they show they can handle it, back off and give them space to do the job the way they see fit.
- Give subordinates as much background information as possible. Let them know *why* things need to be done and how their jobs fit into the overall picture.
- If employees persist in undesirable behavior, persist in telling them about it. Confront them with the problem and try to get to the real reason behind their insubordination.
- When it becames obvious that the employee is *not* going to change, even when confronted with the possibility of dismissal—fire him or her as quickly as possible.

• Involve your subordinates in problem solving and decision making whenever their input might be useful and the decisions concern their work.

• Don't ask for a subordinate's opinion unless you're really willing to listen.

11 How to Take an Assertive Stand With Your Boss

• Remember that the worst possible consequence of speaking up is that you might lose the job—and that is *not* the end of the world.

• You can say almost anything to your boss if you do it properly: a) Consider his point of view; b) Talk straight; c) Speak in a nonthreatening, conversational tone; d) Have the background facts and presentation clear in your own mind first.

• Always check out rumors thoroughly. Don't jump to conclusions or attempt to read your boss's mind.

• Accept the blame for your errors. Let the boss know you're willing to correct them, and ask for his help if necessary.

• If the boss criticizes you unjustly, tactfully point out his mistake when the two of you are alone. But don't be picky on this issue; if the point is minor, let it pass. The important thing is to show the boss that you care about end results as much as he does.

• When you want something, ask for it in a direct, positive way. Back up your requests with benefits, reasons, and a plan all worked out to make it as simple as possible for your boss to grant it.

• Avoid negative language: "I don't know if you can help me, but . . ." "It's probably too much to ask, but . . ."

• If you want to be paid more money, ask for it. Time your request to coincide with your boss's good mood, an appropriate review time, and your own outstanding performance. Be specific as to the amount you want. Have some reasons to back up your request.

• When you get what you wanted, or something close to it, thank the person responsible for your getting it.

• Negotiate hard in the negotiating room, but accept the results amiably. Don't hold grudges.

12 To Women in Management

• Work on changing men's offensive *behavior,* not their attitudes and beliefs.
• Tell men what you want. Tell them what's bothering you.
• Deflect criticism by agreeing with the truth in it. If you care what the person thinks, probe for feedback. Reassure them that you are not a man-hater.
• Don't impugn motives or try to read minds. Unless there is proof to the contrary, assume the best intentions and act accordingly.
• Don't let bad feelings build up. Speak up at once to the person directly responsible for the situation bothering you.
• Don't complain about a superior to co-workers and subordinates. Take your complaints to the source.
• Be persistent. Don't give up the first time you don't get what you ask for.
• Back up your requests with good reasoning. Go in with a plan.
• Don't get emotional. Wait until you've calmed down. Take a few deep breaths. Talk in a calm, conversational manner.
• Don't expect preferential treatment because you're a woman. Learn to take your lumps.
• When someone criticizes your work, try to learn from it. Own up to your mistakes simply and quickly, without exaggerated apologies.
• Relax. You don't have to be perfect. Nobody else is, either.

13 To Men About Women in Management

• Don't try to read a woman's mind. *Ask* her. Get the facts. Speak up when something is bothering you.
• Level with the women you work with. Talk straight.
• Work on one specific problem at a time. Talk

about actual recent behavior, things that can be changed.

• Expect as much from women as you do from men. Give them the same responsibilities and challenges. Criticize them when it is appropriate. Forget the kid-glove handling.

• The women you work with may not want to be treated in the same manner you treat your wife, mother, daughters, etc. Look at your own behavior to see where it might be creating problems with the women you work with.

• If you feel there is trouble between you and a woman subordinate, co-worker, or superior, try to get to the bottom of it. Use nondirective listening, empathy, to get the woman to level with you. Express your own feeling and needs. Try to work out a compromise that will benefit both of you.

• Give women a chance. You'll be glad you did.

Assertiveness Training Workshops

The best way to develop assertive communication skills is to practice them, either in role play or in real-life situations. You can, of course, do so on your own with this book as a guide. But you may also find a workshop helpful for the support, insight, and feedback that a group provides.

Assertiveness training is so popular today that workshops are being held all across the country. To find out where they are given, good places to contact are your local night school, college extension divisions, women's groups, men's and women's "Y's," and other organizations. In addition, your local mental health board or clinic should be able to recommend therapists who specialize in assertiveness training.

While these groups deal with general or personal assertiveness and cover problems with people's spouses, children, friends, etc., you can ask that time also be spent on work-related problems with bosses, peers, and subordinates.

Business realizes the potential value of assertiveness training for managers. This is attested by the fact that various business organizations and management associations now offer seminars in assertiveness for managers and report that managers from numerous companies of all sizes are attending.

In a workshop or seminar you get a chance to talk about actual conflicts and problems you have experienced on the job. The group discussions help you to see things in a different—and probably more objective—perspective, and to come up with appropriate responses to a particular situation.

You'll also get a chance to play roles in the group, thereby trying out the various assertive techniques. People will give you feedback on how you come across —not only your actual words, but their tone and your body language as well.

The other benefit of a workshop is the support system. This is especially true of a continuing group that meets periodically. Instead of facing a conflict alone, you know the group supports you—that they'll cheer you when you succeed and help you figure out what went wrong when you don't.

One of the goals of most assertiveness training workshops is to help people develop a better self-image. There will be exercises to help you develop your confidence and self-respect.

appendix C

For Further Reading

If you wish to delve into a particular subject area more deeply, we've divided the areas researched in connection with this book into the following categories: assertiveness; body language; communication theory; management theory; and miscellaneous. The books and articles listed here offer many valuable ideas, insights, and suggestions. We believe they will repay you for the time you invest in them.

I ASSERTIVENESS

Alberti, Robert E., and Emmons, Michael L. *Stand Up, Speak Out, Talk Back.* Pocket Books, 1975.

——. *Your Perfect Right.* Impact, 1970.

Bloom, Lynn Z., Coburn, Karen, and Pearlman, Joan. *The New Assertive Woman.* Dell Publishing Co., 1975.

Fensterheim, Herbert, and Baer, Jean. *Don't Say Yes When You Want to Say No.* Dell Publishing Co., 1975.

Pellegrino, Victoria. "How to Negotiate for More Status More Money." *Working Woman,* May 1977.

Smith, Manuel J. *When I Say No, I Feel Guilty.* Bantam Books, 1975.

II BODY LANGUAGE

Davis, Flora. *Inside Intuition.* New American Library, 1971.

Fast, Julius. *Body Language.* Pocket Books, 1970.

Nierenberg, Gerard I., and Calero, Henry H. *How to Read a Person Like a Book.* Pocket Books, 1971.

Whiteside, Robert L. *Face Language.* Pocket Books, 1975.

III COMMUNICATION THEORY

Chase, Stuart. *Power of Words*. Harcourt Brace & Co., 1953.

Flesch, Rudolf. *How to Write, Speak, and Think More Effectively*. Harper & Row, 1946.

Genfan, Herb. "Managerial Communication." *Personnel Journal,* November 1976.

Hayakawa, S. I. *Language in Thought and Action*. Harcourt Brace & World, 1939.

McIntosh, Donald W. *Techniques of Business Communication*. Holbrook Press, 1972.

Nierenberg, Gerard I., and Calero, Henry. *Meta Talk*. Pocket Books, 1975.

IV MANAGEMENT THEORY

Burger, Chester. *Creative Firing*. Collier Books, 1972.

McGregor, Douglas. *The Human Side of Enterprise*. McGraw-Hill, 1960.

Peter, Laurence J. *The Peter Prescription*. Bantam Books, 1972.

Townsend, Robert. *Up the Organization*. Alfred A. Knopf, 1970.

Uris, Auren. *The Executive Deskbook*. Van Nostrand Reinholt Co., 1970.

V MISCELLANEOUS

Bootzin, Richard R. *Behavior Modification and Therapy*. Winthrop Publishers, 1975.

Bry, Adelaide. *est—erhard seminars training*. Avon Books, 1976.

Gottlieb, Annie. "Risk Taking: Plunging Into Life." *Working Woman,* April 1977.

Shostrom, Everett L. *Man the Manipulator*. Bantam Books, 1967.

LYN TAETZSCH is an editor for Economics Press in Fairfield, N.J. She has taught business management in colleges and universities and previously was a training manager at Blue Cross-Blue Shield. She has contributed articles to the ASTD *Training & Development Journal* and *Harper's Bazaar* and has written several books, including *Practical Accounting for Small Businesses, Opening Your Own Retail Store,* and *Out of Work: The Complete Job Hunter's Guide.*

EILEEN BENSON is Director of Continuing Education at Felician College in Lodi, N.J. She is also an assertiveness trainer and career counselor; she has conducted workshops and seminars at numerous colleges and universities, as well as for a variety of national organizations and professional groups.

Ms. Benson is presently developing assertiveness training workshops for managers to be given through The Center for Human Development, Mountain Lakes, N.J.